Lessons on Faith

A Selection of Articles and Sermons

A. T. Jones and E. J. Waggoner

World rights reserved. This book or any portion thereof may not be copied or reproduced in any form or manner whatever, except as provided by law, without the written permission of the publisher, except by a reviewer who may quote brief passages in a review.

The author assumes full responsibility for the accuracy of all facts and quotations as cited in this book. The opinions expressed in this book are the author's personal views and interpretations, and do not necessarily reflect those of the publisher.

This book is provided with the understanding that the publisher is not engaged in giving spiritual, legal, medical, or other professional advice. If authoritative advice is needed, the reader should seek the counsel of a competent professional.

_____

Copyright © 1995, 1999, 2015 TEACH Services, Inc.

ISBN-13: 978-1-4796-0514-9 (Paperback)

ISBN-13: 978-1-4796-0515-6 (ePub)

ISBN-13: 978-1-4796-0516-3 (Mobi)

Library of Congress Control Number: 2015934429

Published by

www.TEACHServices.com • (800) 367-1844

TABLE OF CONTENTS

Foreword 5
Living By Faith 7
Lessons On Faith 11
For Our Sake Also 30
Creation Or Evolution, Which? 32
Saving Faith 42
Christ—The End Of The Law 44
The Unconquerable Life 46
Faith 48
Boundless Grace—Free To All 51
Shall It Be Grace Or Sin? 53
Receive Not The Grace Of God In Vain 55
Sinful Flesh 58
A Dead Formalism–I 60
A Dead Formalism–II 63
Ministers Of God 65
Kept By The Word 67
The Power Of The Word–I 69
The Power Of The Word–II 71
Living By The Word 73
Studies In Galatians 76
    Galatians 2:20 78
    Galatians 3:10–12 80
    Galatians 5:3 82
    Galatians 5:16–18 85
    Galatians 5:22–26 88
Christian Perfection 91

FOREWORD

During the last part of the nineteenth century, the Lord brought a message of righteousness to the Church through Elders E. J. Waggoner and A. T. Jones. This message was made prominent in 1888 and for the next decade. It was identified as the beginning of the loud cry of the third angel whose glory was to fill the whole earth.

The loud cry was to go as fire in the stubble. What happened to it? The fact that we are still waiting for the return of Jesus is compelling evidence that this light was not accepted.

In 1895 we were warned that those who were rejecting Christ's delegated messengers and the truth they were bringing were rejecting Christ. Some said, "This is only excitement; it is not the Holy Spirit, not showers of the latter rain from heaven." There were hearts full of unbelief, who did not drink in of the Spirit.

Many years have passed since then. What is our attitude toward the message of righteousness that God sent through Elders Waggoner and Jones? Are we resisting that light, or do we even know what it is?

We believe that the light the Lord gave through Elders Waggoner and Jones has been unknown for a great many years. But now once again the Lord has sent His Holy Spirit to bring this light to the church.

Our purpose in this book is to make available more of the writings of Elders Waggoner and Jones. The Lord has sent light to break the power of Satan in the life and to bring in everlasting righteousness. Let us ask Him for hearts full of belief in Jesus, that we will drink in of His Spirit, and joyfully receive the light which is to fill the whole earth with its glory.

LIVING BY FAITH

E. J. WAGGONER

"The just shall live by faith." Rom. 1:17.

This statement is the summing up of what the apostle has to say about the gospel. The gospel is the power of God unto salvation, but only "to every one that believeth;" in it the righteousness of God is revealed. The righteousness of God is the perfect law of God, which is but the transcript of his own righteous will. All unrighteousness is sin, or the transgression of the law. The gospel is God's remedy for sin; its work, therefore, must be to bring men into harmony with the law,—to cause the workings of the righteous law to be manifested in their lives. But this is wholly a work of faith,—the righteousness of God is revealed from "faith to faith"—faith in the beginning, and faith to the end,—as it is written, "The just shall live by faith."

This is true in all ages since the fall of man, and will be true until the saints of God have his name in their foreheads, and see him as he is. It was from the prophet Habbakuk (2:4) that the apostle quoted the statement. If the prophets had not revealed it, the first Christians could not have known of it; for they had only the Old Testament. To say that in the most ancient times men had but an imperfect idea of faith in Christ, is to say that there were no just men in those times. But Paul goes right back to the very beginning and cites an instance of saving faith. He says: "By faith Abel offered unto God a more excellent sacrifice than Cain, by which he obtained witness that he was righteous." Heb. 11:4. He says of Noah, also, that it was by faith that he built the ark to the saving of his house; "by the which he condemned the world, and became heir of the righteousness which is by faith." Heb. 11:7. We say that their faith was in Christ, because it was faith unto salvation, and besides the name of Jesus "there is none other name under heaven given among men, whereby we must be saved." Acts 4:12.

There are too many who try to live the Christian life on the strength of the faith which they exercised when they realized their need of pardon for the sins of their past life. They know that God alone can pardon sins, and that he does this through Christ; but they imagine that having once been started they must run the race in their own strength. We know that many have this idea, first, because we have heard some say so, and second, because there are such multitudes of professed Christians who show the working of no greater power than their own. If they ever have anything to say in social meeting, besides the ever-recurring formula, "I want to be a Christian, so that I may be saved," they tell only of a past experience, of the joy they had when they first believed. Of the joy of living for God, and of walking with him by faith, they know nothing, and he who tells of it speaks a strange language to them. But the apostle carries this matter of faith clear through to the glorious kingdom, in the following most forcible illustration:—

"By faith Enoch was translated that he should not see death; and was not found, because God had translated him; for before his translation he had this testimony that he pleased God. But without faith it is impossible to please him; for he that cometh to God must believe that he is, and that he is a rewarder of them that diligently seek him." Heb. 11:5, 6.

Note the argument to prove that Enoch was translated by faith: Enoch was translated because he walked with God, and had the testimony that he pleased God; but without faith it is impossible to please God. That is enough to prove the point. Without faith not an act can be performed that will meet the approval of God. Without faith the best deeds that a man can do will come infinitely short of the perfect righteousness of God, which is the only standard. Wherever real faith is found it is a good thing; but the best of faith in God to take away the load of the sins of the past will profit a person nothing unless it is carried right through in ever-increasing measure until the close of his probation.

We have heard many people tell how hard they found it to do right; their Christian life was most unsatisfactory to them, being marked only by failure, and they were tempted to give up in discouragement. No wonder they get discouraged; continual failure is enough to discourage anybody. The bravest soldier in the world would become faint-hearted if he had been defeated in every battle. Sometimes these persons will mournfully tell that they have about lost confidence in themselves. Poor souls, if they would only lose confidence in themselves entirely, and would put their whole trust in the one who is mighty to save, they would have a different story to tell. They would then "joy in God through our Lord Jesus Christ." Says the apostle, "Rejoice in the Lord always; and again I say, Rejoice." Phil. 4:4. The man who doesn't rejoice in God, even though tempted and afflicted, is not fighting the good fight of faith. He is fighting the poor fight of self-confidence and defeat.

All the promises of final happiness are to the overcomer. "To him that overcometh," says Jesus, "will I give to sit with me in my throne, even as I also overcame, and am set down with my Father in his throne." Rev. 3:21. "He that overcometh shall inherit all things," says the Lord. Rev. 21:7. An overcomer is one who gains victories. The inheriting is not the overcoming; that is only the reward for overcoming. The overcoming is now; the victories to be gained are victories over the lusts of the flesh, the lusts of the eyes, and the pride of life, victories over self and selfish indulgences. The man who fights and sees the foe give way, may rejoice; nobody can keep him from rejoicing, for joy comes spontaneously as the result of seeing the enemy give way. Some folks look with dread upon the thought of having to wage a continual warfare with self and worldly lusts. That is because they do not as yet know anything about the joy of victory; they have experienced only defeat. But it isn't so doleful a thing to battle constantly, when there is continual victory. The old veteran of a hundred battles, who has been victorious in every fight, longs to be at the scene of conflict. Alexander's soldiers, who under his command never knew defeat, were always impatient to be led into the fray. Each victory increased their strength, which was born only of courage, and correspondingly diminished that of the vanquished foe, Now how may we gain continual victories in our spiritual warfare? Listen to the beloved disciple:—

"For whatsoever is born of God overcometh the world; and this is the victory that overcometh the world, even our faith." 1 John 5:4.

Read again the words of the apostle Paul:—

"I am crucified with Christ; nevertheless I live; yet not I, but Christ liveth in me; and the life which I now live in the flesh I live by the faith of the Son of God, who loved me, and gave himself for me." Gal. 2:20.

Here is the secret of strength. It is Christ, the Son of God, the one to whom all power in Heaven and earth is given, who does the work. If he lives in the heart to do the work, is it boasting to say that continual victories may be gained? Yes, it is boasting; but it is boasting in the Lord, and that is allowable. Says the psalmist, "My soul shall make her boast in the Lord;" and Paul says: "God forbid that I should glory save in the cross of our Lord Jesus Christ, by whom the world is crucified unto me, and I unto the world." Gal. 6:14.

The soldiers of Alexander were reckoned invincible. Why? Was it because they were naturally stronger and more courageous than all their enemies? No; but because they were led by Alexander. Their strength was in his leadership. Under another leader they would often have been defeated. When the Union army was fleeing panic-stricken, before the enemy at Winchester, the presence of Sheridan turned their defeat into victory. Without him the men were a quaking mob; with him at their head they were an invincible army. If you had listened to the remarks after the battle, of the soldiers who served under those and similar leaders, you would have heard the praises of their general mingled with all their rejoicing.

They were strong because he was; they were inspired by the same spirit that he had.

Well, our captain is the Lord of hosts. He has met the chiefest foe of all and has vanquished him single-handed. Those who follow him invariably go forth conquering and to conquer. Oh, that those who profess to be his followers would put their trust in him, and then, by the repeated victories that they would gain, they would show forth the praises of Him who has called them out of darkness into his marvelous light.

John says that he that is born of God overcomes the world, through faith. Faith lays hold of the arm of God, and his mighty power does the work. How the power of God can work in a man, accomplishing that which he could not possibly do for himself, no one can tell. It would be as easy to tell how God can give life to the dead. Says Jesus: "The wind bloweth where it listeth, and thou hearest the sound thereof, but canst not tell whence it cometh and whither it goeth; so is everyone that is born of the Spirit." John 3:8. How the Spirit works in a man to subdue his passions, and to make him victorious over pride, envy, and selfishness, is known only to the Spirit; it is sufficient for us to know that it is done, and will be done in everyone who wants that work wrought in him, above all things else, and who trusts God for the performance of it.

We cannot tell how Peter was enabled to walk on the water, when the waves were rolling about him; but we know that at the command of the Lord he did it. So long as he kept his eye fixed on the Master, divine power enabled him to walk as easily as though it were solid rock underneath; but when he looked at the waves, possibly with a feeling of pride in what he was doing, as though he himself was doing it, fear very naturally took possession of him, and he began to sink. Faith enabled him to walk on the waves; fear made him sink beneath them.

Says the apostle: "By faith the walls of Jericho fell down after they were compassed about seven days." Heb. 11:30. Why was that written? For our learning, "that we through patience and comfort of the Scriptures might have hope." Rom. 15:4. Why, is there any prospect that we shall ever be called upon to fight armed hosts, and to take fortified cities? No; "for we wrestle not against flesh and blood, but against principalities, against powers, against the rulers of the darkness of this world, against spiritual wickedness in high places" (Eph. 6:1 2); but the victories which have been gained by faith in God over visible foes in the flesh, are placed on record to show us what faith will accomplish in our conflict with the rulers of the darkness of this world. The grace of God, in answer to faith, is as powerful in these battles as in those; for says the apostle:—

"For though we walk in the flesh, we do not war after the flesh; for the weapons of our warfare are not carnal, but mighty through God to the pulling down of strongholds; casting down imaginations, and every high thing that exalteth itself against the knowledge of God, and bringing into captivity every thought to the obedience of Christ." 2 Cor. 10:3–5.

It was not physical foes alone that faith enabled the ancient worthies to conquer. We read of them that they not only "subdued kingdoms," but "wrought righteousness, obtained promises," and, most wonderful and most encouraging of all, *"out of weakness were made strong."* Heb. 11:33, 34. Their very weakness became strength to them through faith, because the strength of Christ is made perfect in weakness. Who, then, shall lay anything to the charge of God's elect? since it is God that justifieth, and we are his workmanship, created in Christ Jesus unto good works. "Who shall separate us from the love of Christ? shall tribulation, or distress, or persecution, or famine, or nakedness, or peril, or sword?" "Nay, in all these things we are more than conquerors through Him that loved us." Rom. 8:35, 37.

Signs of the Times [ST] March 25, 1889

LESSONS ON FAITH

A. T. JONES

Without faith it is impossible to please God. The reason for this is that "whatsoever is not of faith is sin" (Rom. 14:23); and of course sin can not please God.

This is why it is that, as stated by the Spirit of prophecy on the first page of the *Review*, Oct. 18, 1898, "The knowledge of what the Scripture means when urging upon us the necessity of cultivating faith, is more essential than any other knowledge that can be acquired."

And for this cause we shall hereafter, in this place in each number of the *Review* give a Scripture lesson on faith,—what it is, how it comes, how to exercise it,—that every reader of this paper may have this knowledge that "is more essential than any other knowledge that can be acquired."

Review & Herald [RH] Nov. 29,1898

In order to be able to know what the Scripture means when urging upon us the necessity of *cultivating* faith, it is essential to know, first of all, *what is faith*.

Plainly, it must be to little purpose to urge upon a person the necessity of cultivating faith, while that person has no intelligent idea of what faith is. And it is sadly true that, though the Lord has made this perfectly plain in the Scriptures, there are many church members who do not know what faith is. They may even know what the *definition of* faith is: but they do not know what the *thing* is; they do not grasp the idea that is in the definition.

For that reason, the definition will not be touched now; but, rather, there will be cited and studied an illustration of faith, an instance which makes it stand out so plainly that all can see the very thing itself.

Faith comes "by the word of God." To the Word, then, we must look for it.

One day a centurion came to Jesus, and said to him: "Lord, my servant lieth at home sick of the palsy, grievously tormented. And Jesus saith unto him, I will come and heal him. The centurion answered and said, Lord, I am not worthy that thou shouldest come under my roof: but *speak the word only*, and my servant *shall be healed*... When Jesus heard it, he marveled, and said to them that followed, Verily I say unto you, I have not found so great *faith*, no, not in Israel." Matt. 8:6–10.

There is what Jesus pronounces *faith*. When we find what that is, we have found faith. To *know* what that is, is to know what faith is. There can be no sort of doubt about this; for Christ is "the Author...of faith," and he says that that which the centurion manifested was "faith;" yes, even "great faith."

Where, then, in this is the faith? The centurion wanted a certain thing done. He wanted the Lord to do it. But when the Lord said, "I *will come*" and do it, the centurion checked him, saying, *"Speak the word only,"* and it shall *be done.*

Now, what did the centurion expect would do the work *"The word ONLY."* Upon what did he depend for the healing of his servant?—Upon *"the word ONLY.*

And the Lord Jesus says that *that is faith.*

Now, brother, sister, what is faith?

RH Dec. 6, 1898

Faith is the expecting the word of God to do what it says, and the depending upon that word to do what it says.

As that is faith, and as faith comes by the word of God, it is plain that the word of God, in order to inculcate faith, must teach that the word has in itself power to accomplish what itself says.

And such is precisely the truth of the matter: the word of God does teach just this, and nothing else; so that it is truly "the faithful word"—the word full of faith.

The greater part of the very first chapter of the Bible is instruction in faith. That chapter has in itself no fewer than six distinct statements that definitely inculcate faith: with the essential connective of the first verse, there are seven.

The inculcation of faith is the teaching that the word of God itself accomplishes the thing which is spoken in that word.

Read, then, the first verse of the Bible: "In the beginning God created the heaven and the earth." *How* did he create them?—"By *the word of the Lord* were the heavens made; and all the host of them by the breath of his mouth.

"For *he spake, and it was.* " Ps. 33:6–9. *Before* he spoke, it was *not: after* he spoke, "it *was."* Only by the *speaking,* it *was.* What caused it to *be?—The word only.*

But darkness was upon all the face of the deep. God wished light to be there; but how could there be light when all was darkness?—Again he spoke: "And God *said,* Let there be light: and there *was* light." Whence came the light?—The word which was spoken, itself produced the light. "The entrance of *thy words* giveth light." Ps. 119:1 30.

There was no firmament, atmosphere. God wished that there should be a firmament. How could it be produced?—"God *said,* Let there be a firmament.... *and it was so.* " Another translation for "it was so" is, "And *thus* it came to pass." What caused the firmament to be? What caused this *thus* to come to pass?—The word only. He *spoke,* and it was so. The word spoken, itself caused the thing to exist.

God next desired that there should be dry land. How Could this be? Again he spoke: "God *said,* Let the waters under the heaven be gathered together unto one place, and let the dry land appear: *and it was so.*

Then there was no vegetation. Whence should this come? Again God spoke: "And God *said,* Let the earth bring forth grass, the herb yielding seed, and the fruit-tree yielding fruit after his kind, whose seed is in itself, upon the earth: *and it was so."*

Again he spoke: "And God *said,* Let there be lights in the firmament of heaven.... *and it was so."*

Again he spoke: "And God *said, Let* the earth bring forth the living creature, ... *and it was so."*

Thus it was that "by the *word* of the Lord" all things were created. He spoke the word only, and it was so: the word *spoken,* itself produced the *thing.*

Thus it was in creation. And thus it was in redemption: he healed the sick, he cast out devils, he stilled the tempest, he cleansed the lepers, he raised the dead, he forgave sins, all by *his word.* In all this, also, "he *spake, and it was."*

And so he is the same yesterday, and today, and forever. Always he is the Creator. And always he does all things *by his word* only. And always he *can* do all things by his word; because it is the very characteristic of the word of *God,* that it is possessed of the divine power by which itself accomplishes the thing which is spoken.

This is why it is that *faith* is the *knowing* that in the word of God there is this power, the *expecting* the word itself to do the thing spoken, and the *depending* upon that word itself to do that which the word speaks.

The teaching of faith is the teaching that such is the nature of the word of God; the teaching of people to *exercise* faith is the teaching them to expect the word of God to do what it says, and to depend upon *it* to do the thing which is by it spoken; the *cultivating* of faith is by practice to cause to grow confidence in the power of the word of God itself to do what in that word is said, and dependence upon that word itself to accomplish what the word says.

And "the knowledge of what the Scripture means when urging upon us the necessity of cultivating faith, is more essential than any other knowledge that can be acquired."

Are You cultivating faith?

RH Dec. 27, 1898

Faith is the expecting the word of God itself to do what the word says, and depending upon that word itself to do what the word says.

When this is clearly discerned, it is perfectly easy to see how it is that "faith is the *substance* of things hoped for, the *evidence* of things not seen."

Since the word of God is imbued with creative power, and so is able to produce *in very substance* the *thing* which that word speaks; and since faith is the expectation that the word itself will do what the word says, and depending on "the word *only"* to do what that word says, it is plain enough that faith is the *substance* of things hoped for.

Since the word of God is in itself creative, and so is able to produce and cause to appear what otherwise would never exist nor be seen; and since faith is the expecting the word of God only to do just that thing, and depending upon "the word only" to do it, it is plain enough that faith is "the evidence of things not seen."

Thus it is that "through *faith* we understand that the worlds were framed by the word of God, so that things which are seen were not made of things which do appear."

He who exercises faith knows that the word of God is creative, and that so it is able to produce the *thing* spoken. Therefore he can *understand,* not *guess,* that the worlds were produced, were caused to exist, by the word of God.

He who exercises faith can *understand* that though before the word of God was spoken, neither the things which are now seen nor the substances of which those things are composed, anywhere appeared, simply because they did not exist; yet *when* that word was spoken, the worlds *were,* simply because that word itself caused them to exist.

This is the difference between the word of God and the word of man. Man may speak; but there is no power in his words to perform the thing spoken: if the thing is to be accomplished which he has spoken, *the man* must *do* something in addition to speaking the word—he must make good his word.

Not so the word of God.

When God speaks, the thing *is.* And it *is,* simply because he has spoken. *It* accomplishes that which he was pleased to speak. It is not necessary that the Lord, as man, must *do* something in addition to the word spoken. He needs not to make his word good: it *is* good. He speaks "the word *only,*" and the thing is accomplished.

And so it is written: "For this cause also thank we God without ceasing, because, when ye received *the word of God,* which ye heard of us, ye received it *not as the word of men,* but as it is in truth, the word of God, *which* effectually *worketh also* in *you* that *believe*" —in you that exercise faith. 1 Thess. 2:13.

This also is how it is that it is "impossible for God to lie." It is not impossible for God to lie only because he *will* not, but also because he *can* not. And he *can* not lie, just *because* he can not: it is impossible. And it is impossible, because when he speaks, the creative energy is in the word spoken; so that "the word only" causes the thing to be so.

Man may speak a word, and it not be so. Thus man can lie; for to speak what is not so, *is* to lie. And man can lie, can speak what is not so, because there is no power in his word itself to cause the thing to be. With God this is impossible: he *can* not lie; for "he spake, and it was;" he speaks, and it is so.

This is also how it is that when the word of God is spoken for a certain time, as in a prophecy for hundreds of years to come, when that time actually has arrived, that word is fulfilled. And it is then fulfilled, not because, apart from the word, God *does* something to fulfill it; but because the word was spoken for that time, and in it is the creative energy which causes the word *at that time* to produce the thing spoken.

This is how it was that if the children had not cried, "Hosanna to the Son of David," the stones would have immediately cried out; and this is how it was that when the third day had come, it was "impossible" that he should be any longer holden of death.

O, the word of God is divine! In it is creative energy. It is "living and powerful." The word of God is self-fulfilling; and to trust it and depend upon it *as such, that* is to exercise faith. "Hast thou faith?"

RH Jan. 3, 1899

"The knowledge of what the Scripture means when urging upon us the necessity of cultivating faith, is more essential than any other knowledge that can be acquired."

Notice that it is the knowledge of what the Scripture means as to the "necessity of *cultivating* faith,"—not particularly *having* faith, but *cultivating it.*

There is not much said in the Scriptures about any necessity of our *having* faith, while very, very much is said about our *cultivating* faith.

The reason of this is that to all people there is *given* faith to begin with: and all they need to do is to *cultivate* faith. Nobody can have *more* faith than is already given him, with*out cultivating* the faith that is already given, And there is nothing known to man that will grow so fast as faith, when it *is* cultivated—"faith groweth exceedingly."

Faith is the expecting that the word of God itself will accomplish what that word says; and the depending upon "the word only" to accomplish what the word says. To cultivate dependence on the word of God, "the word only," itself to do what the word says, is to cultivate faith.

Faith is "the gift of God" (Eph. 2:8); and that it is given to everybody is plainly stated in the Scriptures: "God hath dealt to every man the measure of faith." Rom. 12:3. This measure of faith which "God hath dealt to every man" is the capital with which God endows and starts "every man that cometh into the world;" and every man is expected to trade upon this capital—cultivate it—to the salvation of his soul.

There is no danger of ever lessening this capital *when it is used:* as certainly as it is used at all, it will increase, it will grow exceedingly. And as certainly as it grows, the righteousness, the peace, the joy, of the Lord, are assured to the full salvation of the soul.

Again: faith comes by the word of God. Therefore, it is written: "The word is nigh thee, even in thy mouth, and in thy heart: *that is,* the word of *faith,* which we preach." Rom. 10:8. Thus *faith,* the very *word of faith,* is in the mouth and in the heart of every man.

How is this?—Thus: when the first pair sinned in the garden, they wholly believed Satan; they gave themselves wholly to Satan; they were taken completely captive by him. Then there was perfect agreement and peace between them and Satan, But God did not leave it so; he broke up this agreement, he spoiled this peace. And he did it by his word, saying to Satan: "I will put enmity between thee and the woman, and between thy seed and her seed." Gen. 3:15.

"It is God alone that can continually put enmity between the seed of the woman and the serpent's seed. After the transgression of man, his nature became evil. Then was peace between Satan and fallen man. Had there been no interference on the part of God, men would have formed an alliance against heaven; and in the place of warfare among themselves, carried on nothing but warfare against God. There is no native enmity between fallen angels and fallen men. Both are evil, and that through apostasy; and evil, wherever it exists, will always league against good. Fallen angels and fallen men join in companionship. The wise general of fallen angels calculated that if he could induce men, as he had angels, to join in rebellion, they would stand as his agents of communication with men to league in rebellion against heaven. Just as soon as one separates from God, he has no power of enmity against Satan. The enmity on earth between man and Satan is supernaturally put there. Unless the converting power of God is brought daily to bear upon the human heart, there will be no inclination to be religiously inclined; but men will choose to be the captives of Satan rather than to be free men in Jesus Christ. I say God will put enmity. Man can not put it. When the will is brought into subjection to the will of God, it must be through man's inclining his heart and will to be on the Lord's side."—*Unpublished Testimony.*

This enmity against Satan, this hatred of evil, which God puts in every person by his word, causes each soul to long for deliverance: and the deliverance is found alone in Jesus Christ. Rom. 7:14–25.

Thus this word of God, which plants in each soul enmity against Satan,—this hatred of evil that calls for deliverance, which is found alone in Jesus Christ,—this is the gift of faith to men; this is "the measure of faith" which God has dealt to every man; this is the "word of faith," which is in the mouth and in the heart of every person in the world.

This "is the word of faith, which we preach: That if thou shalt confess with thy mouth the Lord Jesus, and shalt believe in thine heart that God hath raised him from the dead, thou shalt be saved. For with the heart man believeth unto righteousness; and with the mouth confession is made unto salvation." Rom. 10:8–10.

Therefore say not in thine heart, Who shall ascend into heaven, to bring faith to us? Neither say, Who shall descend into the deep; or, Who shall go far off; to find faith and bring it to us?—For "the word is nigh thee, even in thy mouth, and in thy heart: *that is,* the *word of faith,* which we preach." Deut. 30:11–14; Rom. 10:6–8.

Say that: and *exercise* the faith which God *has given* to *you,* as to every other person in the world; for "understanding how to exercise faith, this is the science of the gospel."

RH Jan. 10, 1899

Faith is the depending upon the word of God only, and expecting that word only, to do what the word says.

Justification by faith, then, is justification by depending upon the word of God only, and expecting that word only, to accomplish it.

Justification by faith is righteousness by faith; for justification is the being declared righteous.

Faith comes by the word of God. Justification by faith, then, is justification that comes by the word of God. Righteousness by faith is righteousness that comes by the word of God.

The word of God is *self*-fulfilling; for in creating all things, "he spake, and it was." And when he was on earth, he stilled the raging sea, cleansed the lepers, healed the sick, raised the dead, and forgave sins, all by his word: there, too, "he spake, and it was."

Now, the same One who, in creating, "spake, and it was;" the same One who said, "Let there be light: and there was light;" the same One who on earth spoke "the word only," and the sick were healed, the lepers were cleansed, and the dead lived,—this same One speaks the righteousness of God unto and upon all that believe.

For though all have sinned and come short of the righteousness of God, yet we are "justified freely by his grace through the redemption that is in Christ Jesus: *whom God hath set forth …to declare his righteousness* for the remission of sins that are past, through the forbearance of God."

In creating all things in the beginning, God set forth Christ to declare the word which should cause all things to exist. Christ did speak the word only, and all things were. And in redemption, which is creation over again, God set forth Christ to declare the word of righteousness. And when Christ speaks the word only, it is so. His word, whether in creating or in redeeming, is the same.

"The worlds were framed by the word of God, so that things which are seen were not made of things which do appear." Once there were no worlds, nor was there any of the material which now composes the worlds. God set forth Christ to declare the word which should produce the worlds, and the very material of which they should be composed.

"He spake, and it was." Before he spoke, there were no worlds: after he spoke, the worlds were there. Thus the word of God spoken by Jesus Christ is able to cause that to exist which has no existence before the word is spoken; and which, except for that word, never could have existence.

In this same way precisely it is in man's life. In man's life there is no righteousness. In man there is no righteousness, from which righteousness can appear in his life. But God has set forth Christ to declare righteousness unto and upon man. Christ has spoken the word only, and in the darkened void of man's life there is righteousness to everyone who will receive it. Where, before the word is received, there was neither righteousness nor anything which could possibly produce righteousness, after the word is received, there is perfect righteousness and the very Fountain from which it springs. The word of God received by faith that is, the word of God expected to do what that word says, and depended upon to do what it says—produces righteousness in the man and in the life where there never was any before; precisely as, in the original creation, the word of God produced worlds where there never were any worlds before. He has spoken, and it is so to everyone that believeth: that is, to every one that receiveth. The word itself produces it.

"Therefore being justified [made righteous] by faith [by expecting, and depending upon, the word of God only], we have peace with God through our Lord Jesus Christ." Rom. 5:1. That is so, bless the Lord! And feeding upon this blessed thing is cultivating faith.

RH Jan. 17, 1899

"The knowledge of what the Scripture means when urging upon us the necessity of cultivating faith, is more important than any other knowledge that can be obtained."

Faith is the expecting the word of God to do the thing which that word speaks, and the depending upon the word only to accomplish the thing which that word speaks.

Abraham is the father of all them which be of faith. The record of Abraham, then, gives instruction in faith—what it is, and what it does for him who has it.

What shall we say, then, that Abraham our father, as pertaining to the faith, has found? What saith the Scripture?

When Abram was more than eighty years old, and Sarai his wife was old, and he had no child, God "brought him forth abroad, and said, Look now toward heaven, and tell the stars, if thou be able to number them: and he said unto him, *So shall thy seed be.*"

And Abram "believed in the Lord; and he counted it to him for righteousness." Gen. 15:5, 6. Abram accepted the word of God, and expected by the word what the word said. And in that he was right.

Sarai, however, did not put her expectation upon the word of God only. She resorted to a device of her own to bring forth seed. She said to him, "The Lord hath restrained me from bearing: I pray thee, go in unto my maid; it may be that I may obtain children by her." Gen. 16:2.

Abram, for the moment, swerved from the perfect integrity of faith. Instead of holding fast his expectation and dependence upon the word of God only, he "harkened to the voice of Sarai."

Accordingly, a child was born; but the whole matter proved to be so unsatisfactory to Sarai that she repudiated her own arrangement. And God showed his repudiation of it by totally ignoring the fact that any child had been born. He changed Abram's name to Abraham, and continued to talk about making him the father of nations through the seed promised, and of making his covenant with Abraham and the seed that was promised. He also changed Sarai's name to Sarah, because she should "be a mother of nations" through the promised seed.

Abraham noticed this total ignoring of the child that had been born, and called the Lord's attention to it, saying, "O, that Ishmael might live before thee!"

But "God said, Sarah thy wife shall bear thee a son indeed; and thou shalt call his name Isaac: and I will establish my covenant with him for an everlasting covenant, and with his seed after him. And as for Ishmael, I have heard thee: behold, I have blessed him, and will make him fruitful, and will multiply him exceedingly; twelve princes shall he beget, and I will make him a great nation. *But my covenant* will I establish with Isaac, which Sarah shall bear unto thee at this set time in the next year." Gen. 17:15–21.

By all this, both Abram and Sarai were taught that, in carrying out the promise, the fulfilling of the word of God, nothing would answer but dependence upon that word only. Sarai learned that her device brought only trouble and perplexity, and *delayed the fulfillment of the promise.* Abram learned that in harkening to the voice of Sarai, he had missed the word of God; and that now he must abandon that whole scheme, and turn again to the word of God only.

But *now* Abraham was ninety-nine years old, and Sarah was eighty-nine. And, if anything, this seemed to put farther off than ever the fulfillment of the word, and called for a deeper dependence upon the word of God—a greater faith than before.

It was perfectly plain that *now* there was no possibility of dependence upon anything whatever, but the naked word only: they were shut up absolutely to this for the accomplishment of what the word said, All works, devices, plans, and efforts of their own were excluded, and they were shut up to faith alone,—shut up to the word alone, and to absolute dependence upon that word only for the accomplishment of what that word said.

And now that the way was clear for "the word only" to work, that word did work effectually, and the promised "seed" was born. And so "through faith,"—through helpless, total dependence upon the word only,—"Sarah *herself* received strength to conceive seed, and was delivered of a child when she was past age, because she judged him faithful who had promised."

And "therefore sprang there even of one, and *him as good as dead,* so many as the stars of the sky in multitude, and as the sand which is by the seashore innumerable." Heb. 11:12.

And *thus* was fulfilled the word spoken to Abram, when God "brought him forth abroad, and said, Look now toward heaven, and tell the stars, if thou be able to number them…so shall thy seed be."

This is a divine lesson in faith. And this is what the Scripture means when urging upon *us* the necessity of cultivating faith. For this was imputed to Abraham for righteousness, even the righteousness of God, which is by faith.

Yet "it was not written for his sake alone, that it was imputed to him; but for *us also,* to whom it shall be imputed, if we believe on him that raised up Jesus our Lord from the dead; who was delivered for our offenses, and was raised again for our justification." Rom. 4:23-25.

And all "they which be of faith are blessed with faithful Abraham." All they who, excluding—yea, repudiating—all works, plans, devices, and efforts, of their own, depend in utter helplessness upon the word of God only to accomplish what that word *says,—these* are they which be of faith, and *are* blessed with faithful Abraham *with the righteousness of God.*

O, "understanding how to exercise faith: this is the science of the gospel"! And the science of the gospel is the science of sciences. Who would not strain every nerve to understand it?

RH Jan. 24,1899

When Abraham and Sarah had cleared themselves of all the scheme of unbelief which had produced Ishmael, and had stood upon faith alone,—dependence on the word of God alone,—Isaac, the true child of the promise, was born.

In harkening to the voice of Sarai (Gen. 16:1), Abram had swerved from the line of strict integrity to the word of God, from the strictness of true faith; and now that he had returned to the word only, to true faith, he must be tested before it could be certainly said of him that his faith was counted for righteousness.

He had trusted the naked word of God as against Ishmael, and had obtained Isaac, the true child of the promise of God. And now, having obtained Isaac, the question must be determined whether he would trust the naked word of God as against even Isaac himself.

Accordingly, God said to Abraham, "Take now thy son, thine *only* son Isaac, whom thou lovest, and get thee into the land of Moriah; and offer him there for a burnt-offering upon one of the mountains which I will tell thee of."

Abraham had received Isaac from God, by trusting the word of God only. Isaac alone was the seed promised by the word of the Lord. After Isaac was born, God had confirmed the word by declaring, "In Isaac shall thy seed be called." Gen. 21:12. And now came the word of God, Take thy son, thine only son Isaac, and offer him for a burnt-offering.

God had declared to Abraham, Thy seed shall be as the stars of heaven for multitude; "In thy seed shall all the nations of the earth be blessed;" "In Isaac shall thy seed be called;" and *now*, Offer Isaac for a burnt-offering!

But, if Isaac is offered for a burnt-offering, if Isaac is burned up, what will become of the promise of the blessing of all nations in him? What will become of the promise, Thy seed shall be as the stars of heaven innumerable?ABraham had trusted the word of God only, as against Ishmael; but *this is more* than trusting the word of God as against *Isaac it* is trusting the word of God as against *the word of God!*

And Abraham did it, hoping against hope. God had said: Thy seed shall be as the stars of heaven; In Isaac shall thy seed be called; Offer Isaac for a burnt-offering. Abraham did not insist that God should "harmonize these passages." It was all-sufficient for *him* to know that the statements were all *the word of God*. Knowing this, he would trust that word, would follow that word, and would let the Lord "harmonize these passages," or "explain these texts," if any such thing were needed.

Said Abraham: God has said, Offer Isaac for a burnt-offering. That I will do. God has said, "In Isaac shall thy seed be called;" and, Thy seed shall be as the stars of heaven for multitude. I interfered once in the promise, and hindered it till I repudiated all that I had done, and came back to the word only. *Then,* by a miracle, God gave me Isaac, the promised seed. Now *he* says, Offer Isaac, the promised seed, for a burnt-offering. I will do it: by a miracle God gave him at the first; and by a miracle God can restore him. Yet when I shall have offered him for a burnt-offering, he will be dead; and the only miracle that can then restore him is a miracle that will bring him back from the dead. But God is able to do even that, *and he will do it;* for his word is spoken, Thy seed shall be as the stars of heaven for multitude, and, In Isaac shall thy seed be called. And even the bringing back of Isaac from the dead will be to God no more than he has already done; for, as to offspring, both my body and Sarah's were as good as dead, and yet God brought forth Isaac from us. He can raise Isaac from the dead, and he will. Bless the Lord!

It was settled. He arose, and took his servants and Isaac, and went three days' journey "unto the place of which God had told him. "And when on the third day he "saw the place afar off," "Abraham said unto his young men, Abide ye here with the ass; and I and the lad will go yonder and worship, and come again to you." Gen. 22:5. Who will go?—"I and the lad will go." And who will come again:—"I and the lad will go,...*and come again* to you." Abraham expected to have Isaac *come back* with him as certainly as that he *went* with him.

Abraham expected to offer Isaac for a burnt-offering, and expected *then* to see Isaac rise from the ashes and go back with him. For the word of God had gone forth, In Isaac shall thy seed be called, and, Thy seed shall be as the stars of heaven for multitude. And Abraham would trust that word only, that it *could* never fail. Heb. 11:17-19.

THIS IS FAITH. And thus "the scripture was fulfilled which saith, Abraham believed God, and it was imputed unto him for righteousness." James 2:23. But yet above this, "It was not written for his sake alone, that it was imputed to him; but for us also, to whom it shall be imputed; if we believe on him that raised up Jesus our Lord from the dead; who was delivered for our offenses, and was raised again for our justification." Rom. 4:23-25.

To trust the word of God only; to depend upon the word of God only; to depend upon the word of God, even as against the word of God,—*this* is FAITH: this is the faith which brings the righteousness of God.

This is what it is to *exercise* faith. *This* is "what the Scripture means when urging upon us the necessity of exercising faith." And "understanding how to exercise faith," this is the science of the gospel. And the science of the gospel is the science of sciences.

RH Jan. 31, 1899

"To HIM that worketh not, but believeth on him that justifieth the ungodly, his faith is counted for righteousness." Rom. 4:5.

This is the only way that anybody in this world can ever become righteous: first admit that he is ungodly; then believe that God justifies, counts righteous, the ungodly, and he is righteous with the very righteousness of God.

Everybody in the world is ungodly. "Ungodly" means "unlike God." And it is written, "All have sinned and come short of the glory [the goodness, the character] of God."

Anybody, therefore, who will admit that he ever came short of being like God in anything, in that confesses that he is ungodly.

But the truth is that *everybody,* in *everything,* has come short of being like God. For "they are all gone out of the way, they are together become unprofitable: there is none that doeth good, no, not one." Rom. 3:9-18.

Then, as there is not one on earth who is not ungodly, and as God justifies the *ungodly,* this on God's part makes justification—righteousness, salvation—full, free, and *sure* to *every soul on earth.*

And all that anybody needs to do to make it all sure to himself on his own part, is to accept it—to believe that God does justify, personally and individually, him *who is ungodly.*

Thus, strange as it may sound to many, the only qualification, and the only preparation, for justification is for a person to acknowledge that he is ungodly.

Then, having such qualification, having made such preparation, all that is required of him to *obtain* justification, full, free, and sure, is to believe that God justifies *him,* the ungodly one.

It is quite easy for many to believe that they are ungodly, and even to acknowledge it; but for them to believe that God justifies *them*—that is too much.

And the sole reason why they can not believe that God justifies *them,* is that they are ungodly, *so* ungodly.

If only they could find some good in themselves, or if only they could straighten up and do better, they might have some courage to hope that God would justify them. Yes, they would justify themselves by *works,* and then profess to believe in justification by faith!

But that would be only to take away all ground for justification; for if a man can find good in himself, he has it already, and does not need it from anywhere else. If he can straighten up and do better of himself, he does not need any justification from anywhere else.

It is, therefore, a contradiction in terms to say that I am so ungodly that I do not see how the Lord can justify me. For if I am not ungodly, I do not need to be *made* righteous: I *am* righteous. There is no half-way ground between godliness and ungodliness.

But when a person sees himself so ungodly as to find there no possible ground of hope for justification, it is just there that faith comes in; indeed, it is only there that faith can possibly come in.

For faith is dependence on the word of God *only.* So long as there is any dependence on himself, so long as there is any conceivable ground of hope for any dependence upon anything in or about himself, there can be no faith: so long there is no place for faith, since faith is dependence on "the word only."

But when every conceivable ground of hope of any dependence on anything in or about himself, *is gone,* and is acknowledged to be gone; when everything that can be seen is against any hope of justification, *then* it is that, throwing himself on the promise of God, upon the word only, hoping against hope, faith enters: and by faith he finds justification full and free, all ungodly though he be.

For forever it stands written, "To him that worketh not, but believeth on him that justifieth the ungodly, his faith is counted for righteousness." "Even the righteousness of God which is by faith of Jesus Christ." "Whom God hath set forth…to declare his righteousness for the remission of sins that are past."

This is what it is to exercise faith. Are you exercising faith? For "understanding how to exercise faith: this is the science of the gospel."

RH Feb. 7, 1899

"Being justified by faith, we have peace with God through our Lord Jesus Christ." Rom. 5:1.

Since faith is the depending upon the word of God only, for what that word says, being justified by faith is simply being accounted righteous by depending upon the word only.

And since the word is the word of God, dependence upon the word only is dependence upon God only, in the word. Justification by faith, then, is justification—being accounted righteous by dependence upon God only; and upon him only because he has promised.

We are all altogether sinners,—sinful, and ungodly. We are, therefore, all subject to the judgment of God. Rom. 3:9–19. Yet for all of us there is escape from the judgment of God.

But the only way of escape from the judgment of God is *to trust in God.*

When David had sinned in numbering the people, and so had incurred the exemplary judgment of God, the Lord gave him his choice as to whether there should be seven years' famine, or he should flee three months before his enemies, or there should be three days' pestilence. But David would not choose at all; he deferred it all to the Lord, for *him to* choose: saying, "Let us fall now into the hand of the Lord, for his mercies are great." 2 Sam. 24:11–14.

When depending upon God alone, in his word, for righteousness, we have peace with God; because thus we really obtain righteousness, and "the work of righteousness shall be peace; and the effect of righteousness quietness and assurance forever." Isa. 32:17.

When depending upon God alone in his word, for righteousness we have peace through our Lord Jesus Christ, because "He is our peace, who hath made both" God and man "one," "having abolished in his flesh the enmity" "for to make in himself of twain"—of God and man—"one new man, *so* making peace." Eph. 2:14,15.

Further: when depending upon God alone, in his word, for righteousness, we have peace with God through our Lord Jesus Christ, because God *has* "made peace through the blood of his cross, by him to reconcile all things unto himself;…whether they be things in earth, or things in heaven. And *you*, that were sometime alienated and enemies in your mind by wicked works, yet *now hath* he reconciled in the body of his flesh through death, to present you holy and unblameable and unreproachable in his sight: IF *ye continue in the faith*"—*if* you continue to depend only upon God alone in his word. Col. 1:20–23.

When he has made the way so plain, the justification so complete, and the peace so sure to all, and asks all people only to receive it all by simply accepting it from him, and depending upon him for it, why should not every soul on earth be thus justified, and have the peace of God through our Lord Jesus Christ?

This is "what the Scripture means when urging upon us the necessity of exercising faith." Are *you* exercising faith? Are You justified by faith? Have you righteousness by faith? Have you peace with God through our Lord Jesus Christ?

"Have faith in God." Mark 11:22.

RH Feb. 14, 1899

Faith is complete dependence upon the word of God *only*, for the accomplishment of what that word says.

This being so, it must never for a moment be forgotten that where there is no word of God, there can not be any faith.

This is shown also in the truth that "faith cometh by hearing, and hearing by the word of God." Rom. 10:17. Since faith thus comes indeed by the very word of God itself, it is perfectly plain that where there is no word of God, there can be no faith.

This is beautifully illustrated by an instance in the life of David: because David had it in his heart to build a house unto the Lord, the Lord spoke to him by the prophet Nathan, saying, "The Lord telleth thee that he will make thee an house.... And thine house and thy kingdom shall be established forever before thee: thy throne shall be established forever."

Then David prayed and said, "Now, O Lord God, the word that thou hast spoken concerning thy servant, and concerning his house, *establish it forever,* and do as thou hast said, And let thy name be magnified forever, saying, The Lord of hosts is the God over Israel: and let the house of thy servant David be established before thee.

"For thou, O Lord of hosts, God of Israel, hast revealed to thy servant, saying, I will build thee an house: *therefore hath thy servant found in his heart to pray this prayer unto thee.*

"And now, O Lord God, thou art that God, and thy words be true, and thou hast promised this goodness unto thy servant: *therefore now* let it please thee to bless the house of thy servant, that it may continue forever before thee: *for thou,* O Lord God, *hast spoken it:* and with thy blessing let the house of thy servant be blessed forever." 2 Sam. 7:11–29.

His prayer was altogether of faith, because it was altogether of the word of God: the word of God was the *cause* of it; the word of God was the *basis* of it; and the word of God was *all the hope* of David that the prayer would ever be answered.

He asked according to the will of God, because the will of God was expressed in the word of God. Having asked according to the plainly stated will of God, David *knew* that his prayer was heard. And knowing that his prayer was heard, David knew that *he had the petition* which he desired of him. 1 John 5:14. Therefore he said, So let it be. And therefore also the answer to that prayer was, and is, and forevermore shall be, sure unto David.

And this was written for *our learning;* that we might know how to pray in faith, and how in prayer to cultivate faith. Therefore, Go and do thou likewise. Because "the knowledge of what the Scripture means when urging upon us the necessity of cultivating faith is more essential than any other knowledge that can be acquired."

RH Feb. 21, 1899

Faith comes by hearing, and hearing by the word of God.

Therefore the word of God is the only means of faith.

Therefore, where there is no word of God, there can not be any faith.

And where the word of God *is,* faith is entire dependence upon that word for the accomplishment of what that word says.

From all this, which is the truth, it is perfectly plain that in order for any one to ask in faith, he must first of all be sure that he has the word of God for what he asks.

Having the word of God for what he asks, he, like David, can find it in his heart to pray with perfect confidence, which is only in perfect faith.

He who thus prays knows that he is asking according to the will of God: for he knows that he has the plain word of God for it.

Therefore he knows that God hears him; and knowing that God hears him, he knows that he *has* the thing for which he has asked; because the sole basis of his hope for it is *the word* which has spoken it, and which is the sole basis of his asking.

The Lord tells us thus to pray; and thus he has made provision for the steady, strong, and continuous growth of faith.

Many people pray, but do not know whether it is the will of the Lord that they should have what they pray for, and so do not know whether they can certainly claim it; and not knowing whether they can claim it, they are all at sea as to whether their prayers are answered or not.

The Lord does not want anybody to move uncertainly. Therefore he has given *his word,* which thoroughly furnishes every one unto all good works, and by which are given all things that pertain unto life and godliness.

And any one who seeks *in the word of God* the things which God has there provided for all, and upon that specific word prays for that thing, thus asking according to the plainly expressed will of God, knows that his prayer is heard, and that he *has* the thing for which he prayed,

So doing, the prayers will be always certain, the life will be filled with the direct gifts of God, and the faith will be sure and strong, and will be ever increasing in strength.

Many pray the prayer of the disciples, "Lord, increase our faith." This is well. Yet along with this, it must never be forgotten that faith comes only by the word of God. Therefore, as certainly as your faith shall be increased, it can be only by there being in you an increase of the word of God, And the only way that there can be in you an increase of the word of God, is by your harkening to that word, praying to the Lord for the thing which that word says, depending wholly upon that word for that thing, and thanking him that you *have received* it. Then and thus that word is received by you, and lives in you.

Thus while we can pray, "Lord, increase our faith," at the same time we must remember that we are to build up ourselves on our most holy faith. Jude 20.

This is how to exercise faith. Faith can be exercised only on the word of God, and by the word of God; for where there is no word of God, there can not be any faith.

And "understanding how to exercise faith, this is the science of the gospel."

RH Feb. 28, 1899

"The just shall live by faith."

Who are the just?—They are only those who are of faith; because men are justified only by faith.

For though we all "have sinned, and come short of the glory of God," yet we are "justified freely by his grace through the redemption that is in Christ Jesus."

For "to him that worketh is the reward not reckoned of grace, but of debt. But to him that worketh not, but believeth on him that justifieth the ungodly, his faith is counted for righteousness."

"Therefore being justified by faith, we have peace with God through our Lord Jesus Christ." Those who are of faith, and those alone, are the just in the earth.

Now faith is entire dependence on the word of God, that that word shall accomplish what that word says. "It shall accomplish that which I please." Isa. 55:11.

To be justified by faith, then, is to be justified by entire dependence upon the word of God. The just are those who are of the word of God. This is how men become just.

Men must not only *become* just by *faith,*—by dependence upon the word of God,—but *being just,* we must *live* by faith. The just man *lives* in precisely the same way, and by precisely the same thing, that he becomes just.

We become just by faith; faith is entire dependence on the word of God. We, being just, must live by precisely the same thing by which we become just; that is, by entire dependence upon the word of God.

And this is exactly what Jesus said: Man shall live "by *every word that proceedeth out of the mouth of God.*" When Jesus said that, it is perfectly plain that he simply said, in other words, Man shall live by faith.

There is no other way truly to live than by faith, which is simply living by the word of God. Without faith, without the word of God, men only die.

Indeed, without the word of God everything only dies; for in the beginning everything came by the word of God. The word of God is the origin and life of everything; for, "He spake, and it was."

All things animate and inanimate,—sun, moon, and stars, animals and men,—all are entirely dependent upon the word of God for existence. Only in the case of men, God has bestowed upon them the wondrous gift of choice as to whether they will do so or not. This gift opens the door of faith. And when a man does choose to live by the word of God, which is the only means of life, faith—entire dependence upon the word of God—is the means by which he lays hold on the means of life.

Thus "the just shall live by faith," and thus "whatsoever is not of faith is sin;" which is simply to say, The just must live by the word of God; and whatsoever is not of the word of God is sin.

"We can not have a healthy Christian experience, we can not obey the gospel unto salvation, until the science of faith is better understood; and until more faith is exercised."

"Hast thou faith?" Have the faith of God. Here are they that *keep "the faith of Jesus."*

RH Mar. 7,1899

The righteousness of God is revealed to faith. Rom. 1:17.

Faith is complete dependence upon the word of God, expecting that word to do what the word itself says.

Is there, then, righteousness spoken by the word of God, so that people can depend completely upon that word, that the word shall accomplish what the word says?

There is. Indeed, that is the very object of the gift of Christ. For him "God hath set forth…to declare his righteousness for the remission of sins that are past, through the forbearance of God." Rom. 3:25.

Seeing then that God hath set forth Christ expressly to declare, *to speak,* the righteousness of God, it is certain that the word of God has been spoken, upon which there can be complete dependence, expecting that word to do what that word says. In other words, there is righteousness that can be received by faith.

Wherein is this word spoken? It is spoken in the word "forgiveness." "He is faithful and just to forgive us our sins;" "there is forgiveness with thee."

Now what is the meaning of "forgive"? The word "forgive" is composed of "for" and "give," which otherwise is give for. To forgive, therefore, is simply to give for. For the Lord to forgive sin, is to give for sin. But what does the Lord give for sin?—He declares "his *righteousness* for the remission of sins."

Therefore when the Lord forgives—gives for—sin, he gives righteousness for sin. And as the only righteousness that the Lord has is his own, it follows that the only righteousness that God gives, or can give, for sin is the righteousness of God.

This is the righteousness of God as a gift. As all men have only sinned, and, if they are ever clear, must have forgiveness entirely free, and as the forgiveness of sin—the righteousness of God given for sin is entirely free,— this is the righteousness of God as a free gift "upon all men unto justification of life." Rom. 5:18.

Every soul, therefore, who ever asks God for forgiveness of sin, in that very thing asks God to give him righteousness for sin. Every soul who asks God for forgiveness, asks it solely upon the word of God, which speaks forgiveness. And faith is entire dependence upon the word for what the word speaks. Thus righteousness is altogether of faith.

"Every one that asketh receiveth." You have asked the Lord many a time to forgive your sins; that is, you have asked him to give for your sin. But when you ask the Lord to give for your sin, in that you ask him to give the only thing that he does or can give for sin, which is righteousness. That is what it is to ask forgiveness of the Lord.

And he does forgive—he does give for—your sins when you ask him. He *says* he does, and *he does.* "He is faithful—'that is, he will never fail'—and just to forgive us our sins." And the only thing he gives for sins is his righteousness.

Then why not thank him for the righteousness that he freely gives for your sins, when you ask him to?

Do you not see that righteousness by faith is just as plain and simple as the asking God for forgiveness of sin? Indeed, it is just that.

To believe that righteousness is given you for your sin, when you ask forgiveness; and thankfully to receive that righteousness as the gift of God,—this is what it is to exercise faith.

Yet how true it is that "we suffer much trouble and grief because of our unbelief, and of our ignorance of how to exercise faith."

"Hast thou faith?" Have the faith of God. "Here are they that keep…the faith of Jesus."
RH Mar. 14, 1899

"In Jesus Christ neither circumcision availeth anything, nor uncircumcision; but faith which worketh by love." Gal. 5:6.

With those who were in mind when this scripture was originally written, circumcision was everything; and it was everything simply because of what it represented.

And what circumcision represented to those people was works, and works only. It was the greatest of all works,—greater than creation itself,—because, as the rabbis put it, "So great is circumcision, that but for it the Holy One, blessed be he, would not have created the world." "It is as great as all the other commandments;" "equivalent to all the commandments of the law."—*Farrar's "Life of Paul," chap. 22, par. 5, note; chap. 35, par. 4, note.*

Yet this which to them was so great, the Lord sweeps away, as with a blast, in the words, "Circumcision is nothing;" and in Christ Jesus, circumcision avails nothing. And, in view of what circumcision meant to them, this was simply to say that works are nothing, and in Christ Jesus works avail nothing.

Then to all the others, who, in view of this, might be inclined to boast in their lack of works, and thus excuse sin, the word is given with equal force: "And uncircumcision is nothing;" "In Jesus Christ neither…uncircumcision availeth anything:" which, in its connection, was simply to say that the absence of works is nothing; and in Christ Jesus the absence of works avails nothing.

So, then, works are nothing, and the absence of works is nothing. In Christ Jesus neither works nor the lack of works avails anything.

This word of the Lord, therefore, utterly and forever excludes both classes from all merit, and from all ground of merit, in themselves, or in anything they ever did or did not do.

And this is all as true to-day as ever. To-day, whether persons are out of Christ or in Christ, neither works nor no works avail anything. For it is written: "Are you in Christ? Not if you do not acknowledge yourselves erring, helpless, condemned sinners.… Your birth, your reputation, your wealth, your talents, your virtues, your piety, your philanthropy, or anything else in you or connected with you, will not form a bond of union between your soul and Christ,"—*"Testimony for the Church," No. 31, pages 44, 45.*

What then? Is everybody left in utter emptiness?—No, no! Thank the Lord there is *something* which avails for all, and avails forever. Though it be the everlasting truth that "in Jesus Christ neither circumcision availeth anything, nor uncircumcision," neither works nor no works avail anything; yet it is also the eternal truth that "in Jesus Christ…1-Ellipsis potential problem;Christ…FAITH WHICHFAITH WHICH WORKETH," does avail.

Notice that it is not faith *and* works that avail: it is "faith WHICH worketh." It is faith which *itself* is able to work, and does work,—it is this, and this alone, that avails for anybody, anywhere, at any time.

Faith is only of God; and, working, it works only the works of God. Thus he who, in Christ Jesus, has the "faith *which* worketh," has that which avails to show God manifest in the flesh, working the works of God. And thus "this is the *work of God, that ye believe* on him whom he hath sent."

And so, while you are in Christ, "if there is any good in you, it is wholly attributable to the mercy of the compassionate Saviour.... Your connection with the church, the manner in which your brethren regard you, will be of no avail, unless you believe in Christ. It is not enough to believe *about* him; you must believe *in* him. You must rely wholly upon his saving grace."—*Id., pages 44, 45.*

"Hast thou faith?" Have the faith of God. "Here are they that keep…the faith of Jesus."

RH Mar. 28, 1899

DELIVERANCE

"Walk in the Spirit, and ye shall not fulfill the lust of the flesh." Gal. 5:16.

What a blessed promise! and as sure as it is blessed, to every one who believes.

Think of the lust of the flesh. How all-pervading it is! How stern are its dictates! How oppressive its rule! How dismal is the slavery that it lays upon man!

Everybody has experienced it,—longing to do the good that he would, yet doing only the evil that he hated; having ever a will to do better, but how to perform it, finding not; delighting in the law of God after the inward man, yet finding in his members another law, warring against the law of his mind, and bringing him into captivity to the law of sin which is in his members; and at last, crying out, "O wretched man that I am! who shall deliver me from the body of this death?" Rom. 7:14-24.

Thank the Lord, there is deliverance. It is found in Christ Jesus and in the Spirit of our God. Rom. 7:25; 8:1,2. And the law of the Spirit of life in Christ Jesus having made you free from the law of sin and death, then "walk in the Spirit, and ye shall not fulfill the lust of the flesh." There is not only deliverance from the bondage of corruption: there is also the glorious liberty of the children of God for every soul who receives the Spirit, and walks in the Spirit.

"Walk in the Spirit, and ye shall not fulfill the lust of the flesh."

See the list of the workings of the lust of the flesh: "Adultery, fornication, uncleanness, lasciviousness, idolatry, witchcraft, hatred, variance, emulations, wrath, strife, seditions, heresies, envyings, murders, drunkenness, revelings, and such like." None of these shall you fulfill, over all these things you have the victory, when you walk in the Spirit. It is the faithful word of God.

Is not that a most desirable prospect? Is not such a thing as that worth having? And when it is had for the asking and the taking, then is it not worth asking for and taking?

Accept the deliverance that Christ has wrought out for you. Stand, and stand fast, in the liberty wherewith Christ has made us free.

"Ask, and it shall be given you." "For every one that asketh receiveth." "Receive ye the Holy Ghost." "Be filled with the Spirit;" yea, "Walk in the" "Holy Spirit of God, whereby ye are sealed unto the day of redemption."

RH Mar. 14, 1899

FOR OUR SAKE ALSO

E. J. WAGGONER

The fourth chapter of Romans is one of the richest in the Bible, in the hope and courage which it contains for the Christian. In Abraham we have an example of righteousness by faith, and we have set before us the wonderful inheritance promised to those who have the faith of Abraham. And this promise is not limited. The blessing of Abraham comes on the Gentiles as well as on the Jews; there is none so poor that he may not share it, for "it is of faith, that it might be by grace; to the end the promise might be sure to all the seed."

The last clause of the seventeenth verse is worthy of special attention. It contains the secret of the possibility of our success in the Christian life. It says that Abraham believed "God, who quickeneth the dead, and calleth those things which be not as though they were." This marks God's power; it involves creative power. God can call a thing which is not as though it existed. If a man should do that, what would you call it?—A lie. If a man should say that a thing is, when it is not, it would be a lie. But God cannot lie. Therefore when God calls those things that be not, as though they were, it is evident that that makes them be. That is, they spring into existence at his word. We have all heard, as an illustration of confidence, the little girl's statement that "if ma says so, it's so if it isn't so." That is exactly the case with God. Before that time spoken of as "in the beginning," there was a dreary waste of absolute nothingness; God spoke, and instantly worlds sprang into being. "By the word of the Lord were the heavens made; and all the host of them by the breath of his mouth…For he spake, and it was; he commanded, and it stood fast." Ps. 33:6–9. This is the power which is brought to view in Rom. 4:17. Now let us read on, that we may see the force of this language in this connection. Still speaking of Abraham, the apostle says:—

"Who against hope believed in hope, that he might become the father of many nations, according to that which was spoken, So shall thy seed be. And being not weak in faith, he considered not his own body now dead, when he was about a hundred years old, neither yet the deadness of Sarah's womb; he staggered not at the promise of God through unbelief; but was strong in faith, giving glory to God; and being fully persuaded that, what he had promised, he was able also to perform. And therefore it was imputed to him for righteousness." Rom. 4:18–22.

Here we learn that Abraham's faith in God, as one who could bring things into existence by his word, was exercised with respect to his being able to create righteousness in a person destitute of it. Those who look at the trial of Abraham's faith as relating simply to the birth of Isaac, and ending there, lose all the point and beauty of the sacred record. Isaac was only the one in whom his seed was to be called, and that seed was Christ. See Gal. 3:16. When God told Abraham that in his seed all nations of the earth should be blessed, he was preaching the gospel to him (Gal. 3:8); therefore Abraham's faith in the promise of God was direct faith in Christ as the Saviour of sinners. This was the faith which was counted to him for righteousness.

Now note the strength of that faith. His own body was already virtually dead from age, and Sarah was in a like condition. The birth of Isaac from such a pair was nothing less than the bringing of life from the dead. It was a symbol of God's power to quicken to spiritual life those who are dead in trespasses and sins. Abraham hoped against hope. There was no human possibility of the fulfillment of the promise; everything was against it, but his faith grasped and rested upon the unchanging word of God, and his power to create and to make alive. "And therefore it was imputed unto him for righteousness." Now for the point of it all:—

"Now it was not written for his sake alone, that it was imputed to him; but for us also, to whom it shall be imputed, if we believe on him that raised up Jesus our Lord from the dead; who was delivered for our offenses, and was raised again for our justification." Rom. 4:23–25.

So Abraham's faith was the same that ours must be, and in the same object. The fact that it is by faith in the death and resurrection of Christ that we have the same righteousness imputed to us that was imputed to Abraham, shows that Abraham's faith was likewise in the death and resurrection of Christ. All the promises of God to Abraham were for us as well as for him. Indeed, we are told in one place that they were specially for our benefit. "When God made promise to Abraham, because he could swear by no greater, he sware by himself." "Wherein God, willing more abundantly to show unto the heirs of promise the immutability of his counsel, confirmed it by an oath: that by two immutable things, in which it was impossible for God to lie, *we* might have a strong consolation, who have fled for refuge to lay hold upon the hope set before us." Heb. 6:13,17,18. Our hope, therefore, rests upon God's promise and oath to Abraham, for that promise to Abraham, confirmed by that oath, contains all the blessings which God can possibly give to man.

But let us make this matter a little more personal before leaving it. Trembling soul, say not that your sins are so many and that you are so weak that there is no hope for you. Christ came to save the lost, and he is able to save to the uttermost those that come to God by him. You are weak, but he says, "My strength is made perfect in weakness." 2 Cor. 12:9. And the inspired record tells us of those who "out of weakness were made strong." Heb. 11:34. That means that God took their very weakness and turned it into strength. In so doing he demonstrates his power. It is his way of working. For "God hath chosen the weak things of the world to confound the things which are mighty, and base things of the world, and things which are despised, hath God chosen, yea, and things which are not, to bring to naught things that are; that no flesh should glory in his presence." 1 Cor. 1:27–29.

Have the simple faith of Abraham. How did he attain to righteousness?—By not considering the deadness and powerlessness of his own body, but by being willing to grant all the glory to God, strong in faith that he could bring all things out of that which was not. You, therefore, in like manner, consider not the weakness of your own body, but the power and grace of our Lord, being assured that the same word which can create a universe, and raise the dead, can also create in you a clean heart, and make you alive unto God. And so you shall be a child of Abraham, even a child of God by faith in Christ Jesus.

CREATION OR EVOLUTION, WHICH?

A. T. JONES—RH Feb. 21, 28; Mar. 7, 1899

I am going to speak this afternoon on the Subject of Evolution. I want you to pay close attention, and find out for yourselves whether or not you are evolutionists. First of all, I will read to you what evolution is; then as we follow along, you can see whether or not you are an evolutionist. These statements are all copied from a treatise on evolution, written by one of the chief evolutionists; therefore they are all correct, so far as they go, as definitions:—

"Evolution is the theory that represents the course of the world as a gradual transition from the indeterminate to the determinate, from the uniform to the varied, and which assumes the cause of these processes to be immanent in the world itself that is to be thus transformed."

"Evolution is thus almost synonymous with progress. It is a transition from the lower to the higher, from the worse to the better. Thus progress points to an increased value in existence, as judged by our feelings."

Now notice the particular points in these three sentences: evolution represents the course of the world as a gradual transition from the lower to the higher, from the worse to the better; and assumes that this process is immanent in the world itself thus to be transformed. That is to say, the thing gets better of itself; and that which causes it to get better is *itself*. And this progress marks "an increased value in existence, as judged by our feelings." That is to say, you know you are better, because you feel better. You know there has been progress, because you feel it. Your feelings regulate your standing. Your knowledge of your feelings regulates your progress from worse to better.

Now in this matter of progress from worse to better, have *your* feelings anything to do with it? If they have, what are you? Every one here this afternoon who measures his progress, the value of his experience, by his *feelings,* is an evolutionist: I care not if he has been a Seventh-day Adventist for forty years, he is an evolutionist just the same. And all his Christianity, all his religion, is a mere profession without the fact, simply a form without the power.

Now I read what evolution is, in another way; so that you can see that it is infidelity. Then, if you find yourself an evolutionist, you know at once that you are an infidel: "The hypothesis of evolution aims at answering a number of questions respecting *the beginning, or genesis, of things.*" It "helps to restore the ancient sentiment toward nature as our parent, *and the source of our life.*"

One of the branches of this sort of science, that has done most toward the establishment of the doctrine of evolution, is the new science of geology, which has instituted the conception of vast and unimaginable periods of time in the past history of our globe. These vast and unimaginable periods, as another one of the chief writers on this subject—the author of it indeed—says, "is the indispensable basis for understanding man's origin" in the process of evolution. So that the progress that has been made, has been through countless ages. Yet this progress has not been steady and straight forward from its inception until its present condition. It has been through many ups and downs. There have been many times of great beauty and symmetry; then there would come a cataclysm, or an eruption, and all would go to pieces, as it were. Again the process would start from that condition of things, and build up again. Many, many times this process has been gone through; and that is the process of evolution,—the transition from the lower to a higher, from the worse to the better.

Now, what has been the process of your progress from the worse to the better? Has it been through "many ups and downs"? Has your acquiring of the power to do the good—the good works which are of God—been through a long process of ups and downs from the time of your first profession of Christianity until now? Has it appeared sometimes that you had apparently made great progress, that you were doing well, and that everything was nice and pleasant; and then, without a moment's warning there would come a cataclysm, or an eruption, and all be spoiled? Nevertheless, in spite of all the ups and downs, you start in for another effort: and so through this process, long-continued, you have come to where you are to-day; and in "looking back" over it all, you can mark some progress, you *think*, as *judged by your feelings,—is* that your experience? Is that the way *you* have made progress?

In other words, are you an evolutionist? Don't dodge; confess the honest truth; for I want to get you out of evolutionism this afternoon. There is a way to get out of it: and every one who came into this house an evolutionist can go out a Christian. So if, when I am describing an evolutionist, so plainly that you see yourself, just say so,—admit that it is yourself, and then follow along the steps that God will give you, and that will bring you out of it all. But I say plainly to you that, if that which I have described has been your experience, if that has been the kind of progress that you have made in your Christian life, then you are an evolutionist, whether you admit it or not. The best way, however, is to admit it, then quit it, and be a Christian.

Another phase of it: "Evolution, so far as it goes, looks upon matter as eternal." And "by assuming" this, "the notion of *creation* is eliminated from those regions of existence to which it is applied." Now if you look to yourself for the principle which would assure that progress that must be made in you as certainly as ever you reach the kingdom of God; if you suppose that that is immanent in yourself, and that if you could get it rightly to work, and superintend it properly when it had been thus got to work, it would come out all right,—if thus you have been expecting, watching, and marking your progress, you are an evolutionist. For I read further what evolution is: "It is clear that the doctrine of evolution is directly antagonistic to that of creation…. The idea of evolution, as applied to the formation of the world as a whole, is opposed to that of a direct creative volition."

That is evolution, as defined by those who made it,—that the world came, and all there is of it, of itself; and that the principle that has brought it to the condition in which it is, is immanent in itself, and is adequate to produce all that is. This being so, in the nature of things "evolution is directly antagonistic to creation."

Now as to the world and all there is of it, you do not believe that it all came of itself. You know that you are not an evolutionist as to that; because you believe that God created all things. Every one of you here this afternoon would say that you believe that God *created* all things,—the world and all there is in it. Evolution does not admit that: it has no place for creation.

There is, however, another phase of evolution that professedly is not absolutely antagonistic to creation. Those who made this evolution that I have read to you did not pretend to be anything but infidels,—men without faith,—for an infidel simply is a man without faith. Even though a person pretends to have faith, and does not actually have it, he is an infidel. Of course the word "infidel" is more narrowly confined than that nowadays. The men who made this evolution that I have read to you were that kind of men; but when they spread that kind of doctrine abroad, there were a great number of people who professed to be Christians, who professed to be men of faith, who professed to believe the word of God, which teaches creation. These men, not knowing the word of God for themselves, not knowing it to be the word of God, but their faith being a mere form of faith without the power these men, I say, being charmed with this new thing that had sprung up, and wanting to be popular along with the new science, and really not wanting to forsake altogether the word of God and the ways of faith, were not ready to say that they could get along without God, without creation somewhere, so they formed a sort of evolution with the Creator in it. That phase of it is called theistic evolution,— that is, *God started the thing,* whenever that was; but since that, it has been going on of itself. He started it, and after that it was able of itself to accomplish all that has been done. This, however, is but a makeshift, a contrivance to save appearances,—and is plainly declared by the true evolutionists to be but "a phase of transition from the creational to the evolutional hypothesis." It is evolution only; because there is no half-way ground between creation and evolution.

Whether *you* are one of this kind or not, there are many of them, even among Seventh-day Adventists,—not so many as there used to be, thank the Lord!—who believe that we must have God forgive our sins, and so *start* us on the way all right; but after that we are to work out *our own* salvation with fear and trembling. Accordingly, they do fear, and they do tremble, all the time; but they do not work out any salvation, because they do not have God constantly working *in them,* "both to will and to do of his good pleasure." Phil. 2:12,13.

Now in Heb. 11:3 it is recorded that it is through faith that we understand that the worlds were *framed*—put together, arranged, built—"by *the word of God:* so that things which are seen were not made of things which do appear." The earth which we have was not made of rocks; men were not made of monkeys, apes, and "the missing link;" and apes and monkeys and "the missing link" were not made of tadpoles; and tadpoles were not made of protoplasm originally away back at the beginning. No! "the worlds were framed by *the word of God,* so that things which are seen were not made of things which do appear."

Now why is it that things which are seen were not made of things which do appear?— Simply because the things of which these are made did not appear. And the reason those things did not appear is because they *were not* at all. They did not exist. The worlds were framed by the word of God; and the word of God is of that quality, it has that property about it, which, when the word is spoken, not only causes the *thing* to be, but causes to

CREATION OR EVOLUTION, WHICH? 35

exist the material out of which the thing is made, and of which the thing consists.

You know also the other scripture, that "by the word of the Lord were the heavens made, and all the host of them by the breath of his mouth:...for he spake, and it was." Ps. 33:6–9. Upon this I will ask you a question: How long after he spoke, before the things were? How much time passed, after he spoke, before the thing was? [Voice: "no time."] Not a week?—No. Not six long periods of time?—No. Evolution, even that which recognizes a Creator, holds that indefinite countless ages, or "six long, indefinite periods of time," passed in the formation of the things which are seen, *after he spoke*. But that is evolution, not creation: evolution is by long processes. Creation is by the word spoken.

When God, by speaking the word, had created the world,,,, for this one he said, "Let there be light." Now how much time passed between the words, "Let there be light," and the time when the light came? I want you to understand this matter aright, so that you can find out whether you are an evolutionist or a creationist. Let me ask this again. Were there not six long periods of time between the time when the word was spoken and the accomplishment of the fact? You say No. Was it not a week?—No. Not a day?—No. Not an hour?—No. Not a minute?—No. Nor even a second?—No, indeed. There was not a second between the time when God said, "Let there be light," and the existence of the light. [Voice: "Just as soon as the word was spoken, the light was." [Yes, that is the way it was. I go over it thus minutely, so as to get it firmly fixed in your mind, for fear you will let it go presently, when I ask you something further. Now is it settled that when God said, "Let there be light," there was not a second of time between that and the shining of the light? [Voice: "Yes."] All right. Then the man who allows that any time at all passed between God's speaking and the appearing of the thing, is an evolutionist. If he makes it countless ages upon countless ages, he is simply more of an evolutionist than the one who thinks it took a day; he is the same thing, but more of it.

Next, God said, "Let there be a firmament." And what then?—It was so. Then from the time that God spoke, "Let there be a firmament.... and let it divide the waters from the waters," how long before a firmament was there? Was that done instantly?—Yes. Then the man who holds that there was an indefinite, a very long, period of time between the speaking of the word and the existence of the fact,—what is he?—An evolutionist. If he allows that there was a day, or an hour, or a minute, between the speaking of the word, and the existence of the thing itself, that man does not recognize creation.

When the Lord said, "Let the waters under the heaven be gathered together unto one place, and let the dry land appear;" also when he said, "Let the earth bring forth grass, the herb yielding seed, and the fruit-tree yielding fruit,...it was so." Then God set two great lights in the heavens, and made the stars also; and when he spoke the word, "it was so." He said, "Let the waters bring forth abundantly the moving creature that hath life, the fowl that may fly above the earth in the open firmament;" and it was so. When God said, "Let the earth bring forth the living creature after his kind, cattle, and creeping thing, the beast of the earth after his kind," it was so. When he spoke, it was always so. That is creation.

You see, then, that it is perfectly logical, and reasonable enough, too, for the evolutionists to set aside the word of God, and have no faith in it; for evolution itself is antagonistic to creation. When evolution is antagonistic to creation, and creation is by the word of God, then evolution is antagonistic to the word of God. Of course the genuine, or original, sound evolutionist did not have any place for that word, nor for the half-and-half evolutionists,—those who bring in creation and the word of God to start things. It takes so long a time, such indefinite and indeterminate ages, for evolution to accomplish anything, that it does away with creation.

The genuine evolutionist recognizes that creation must be immediate; but he does not believe in immediate action, and therefore does not believe in creation. Do not forget that creation is immediate, or else it is not creation: if not immediate, it is evolution. So touching again the creation at the beginning, when God speaks, there is in his word the creative energy to produce the thing which that word pronounces. That is creation; and that word of God is the same yesterday, and to-day, and forever; it lives and abides forever; it has everlasting life in it. The word of God is a living thing. The life that is in it is the life of God—eternal life. Therefore it is the word of eternal life, as the Lord Jesus said; and in the nature of things it abides and remains forever. Forever it is the word of God; forever it has creative energy in it.

So when Jesus was here, he said, "The words that I speak unto you, they are spirit, and they are life." The words that Jesus spoke are the words of God. They are imbued with the life of God. They are eternal life, they abide forever; and in them is the creative energy to produce the thing spoken.

This is illustrated by many incidents in the life of Christ, as narrated in the New Testament. I do not need to cite them all; but I will refer to one or two, so you can get hold of this principle. You remember that after the sermon on the mount, Jesus came down, and there met him a centurion, saying, "My servant lieth at home sick of the palsy, grievously tormented. Jesus saith unto him, I will come and heal him." The centurion said: "I am not worthy that thou shouldest come under my roof; but speak the word only, and my servant shall be healed." Jesus turned to those standing about, and said, "I have not found so great faith, no, not in Israel."

Israel had the Bible; they knew the word of God. They boasted of being the people of the Book, the people of God. They read it; they preached in their synagogues, "My word… shall accomplish that which I please." They said, when they read that word: That is all right; the thing ought to be done. We see the necessity of it, and will do it. We will accomplish what it says. Then they did their best to accomplish it. It took them a long while, so long indeed, that they *never* did it. Their real doing of the word was so far away that the greatest of them were led to exclaim, "If but one person could only for one day keep the whole law, and not offend in one point,—nay, if but one person could but keep that one point of the law which affected the due observance of the Sabbath,—then the troubles of Israel would be ended, and the Messiah at last would come." So, though they started in to do what the word said, it took them so long that they never got to it. What were they?

There was the word of God, which said, "*It* shall accomplish that which I please." It was spoken thus of the creative power. And though they professed to recognize the creative energy of the word of God, yet in their own lives they left that all out, and said, *We* will do it. They looked to themselves for the process which would bring themselves to the point where that word and themselves would agree. What were they? Are you afraid to say, for fear you have been there yourself? Do not be afraid to say that they were evolutionists, for that is what they were, and that is what a good many of you are. Their course was antagonistic to creation; there was no creation about it. They were not made new creatures, no new life was formed within them; the thing was not accomplished by the power of God; it was all of themselves; and so far were they from believing in creation that they rejected the Creator, and crucified him out of the world. That is what evolution always does; for do not forget that evolution is directly antagonistic to creation."

Now these were the people upon whom Jesus looked when he made this statement about faith in Israel. Here was a man who was a Roman, who had grown up among the people who were Jews, and who set at naught the teachings of Jesus. That centurion had been around where Jesus was, had seen him talking, had heard his words and had seen the effect of them, until he himself said, Whatever that man speaks is so: when he says a thing, it is done. Now I am going to have the advantage of it. So he went to Jesus, and said what is written. Jesus knew perfectly well that the man had his mind upon the power of his word to do that thing; and he replied, Very well, I will come and heal your servant. O no, my Lord, you do not need to *come*. You see this man was testing the matter, to see whether or not there was any power in the word. Therefore he said, "Speak the word only, and my servant shall be healed." Jesus replied, "As thou hast believed, *so be it* done unto thee. And his servant was healed." When that word went forth, "*so be it* done unto thee," how long before the man was healed? Twenty years?—No. Didn't he have to go through many ups and downs before he was certainly healed? Honest, now?—No, no! When the word was spoken, the word did the thing that was spoken; and it did it *at once.*

Another day Jesus was walking along, and a leper some distance from him saw and recognized him. He, too, had got hold of the blessed truth of the creative energy of the word of God. He said to Jesus, "If thou wilt, thou canst make me clean." Jesus stopped, and said, "I will; be thou clean. And as soon as he had spoken, immediately the leprosy departed from him, and he was cleansed." Mark 1:41,42. We are not allowed to put a moment of time between the speaking of the word and the accomplished fact: *"immediately"* the leper was cleansed.

Now you see that the word of God at the beginning of creation had in it the creative energy to produce that thing which the word pronounced. You see that when Jesus came into the world to show men the way of life, to save them from their sins, he demonstrated, over and over again, here and there and everywhere, to all people and for all time, that that same word of God has that same creative energy in it yet, so that when that word is spoken, the creative energy is there to produce the thing.

Now are you an evolutionist, or are you a creationist? That word speaks to you. You have read it, you profess to believe it. You believe in creation, as against the other evolutionists; now will you believe in creation, as against yourself. Will you put yourself upon that platform to-day where you will allow nothing to come between you and the creative energy of that word—no period of time whatever?

Jesus said to a certain person, "Thy sins are forgiven." How long before it was so?—There was no length of time whatever between the word "forgiven" and the thing. That same word, "Thy sins are forgiven," is spoken to you to-day. Why do you let any time pass between this word, which is spoken to you, and the accomplishment of the thing? You said a while ago, that anybody who let a minute, or even a second, pass between the speaking of the word of God and the production of the thing, is an evolutionist. Very good; that is so. Stick to it. Now I ask you, Why is it that when he speaks forgiveness to you, you let whole days pass before forgiveness gets to you, before it is true in you? You said the other man is an evolutionist. What are you, I want to know? Are you going to stop being evolutionists and become creationists?

This day will be one of special importance to many here, because it is a time when many will decide this question one way or the other. If you go out of this house an evolutionist, you are in danger. It is to you a matter of life or death just now. You said that evolution is infidelity, and that is so; therefore if you go out of this house an evolutionist, where do you stand? What is your choice? And if you go out of this house without the forgiveness of sins, you are an evolutionist, because you allow time to pass between the speaking of the word and the accomplishment of the fact.

From what I have read, you see that whoever lets any time pass between the word spoken and the thing done, is an evolutionist. The word of God to you is, Man, "thy sins are forgiven thee." Woman "thy sins are forgiven thee." [Eider Corliss: "Didn't it say, Thy Sins shall be forgiven?"] No, Sir: "thy Sins *are* forgiven thee,"—present tense, with an emphasis,—"Thy sins *are* forgiven." I thank God this is so, because the creative energy is in that word "forgiven" to take away all sin, and create the man a new creature. I believe in creation. Do you? Do you believe in the creative energy that is in the word "forgiven" spoken to you? Or are you an evolutionist, and do you say, I can not see how that can be, because I am so bad? I have been trying to do right, but I have made many failures: I have had many ups and downs, and have been down a good many more times than up. If that is what you say, you are all evolutionist; for that is evolution.

Many people have been longing and longing for a clean heart. They say: "I believe in the forgiveness of sin and all that, and I would take it all, if I was sure that I could hold out; but there is so much evil in my heart, and so many things to overcome, that I do not have any confidence." But there stands the word, "*Create* in me a clean heart." A clean heart comes by *creation*, and by no other means; and that creation is wrought by the word of God. For he says, "A new heart also will I give you, and a new spirit will I put within you." Are you a creationist now, or are you an evolutionist? Will you go out of this house with an evil heart, or with a new heart, created by the word of God, which has in it creative energy to produce a new heart? It speaks to you a new heart. To every one it speaks just that way; and if you allow a moment to pass between the speaking of the word and the new heart, you are an evolutionist. When you allow any time to pass between the word spoken and the fulfillment of that thing in your experience, then you are an evolutionist,

There are those in this house who have said: Yes, I want it, I am going to have it, I believe the word will accomplish it; but they have lengthened out the time until the next meeting, and on and on, passing over years; and so they are just this much evolutionists. "While so many are hovering about the mystery of faith and godliness, they could have solved the matter by proclaiming [speaking abroad, telling it out] , 'I know that Jesus Christ is my portion forever.' " The power to produce this is in the word of God; and when this is accepted, the creative energy is there producing the thing that is spoken. So you can settle the whole matter of the mystery of faith and godliness by proclaiming that you know that Christ is your portion forever,

There *is* a mystery in how God can be manifest in such sinful flesh as yours. But, mind you, the question is not now about the *mystery*; the question is, Is there such a thing as *creation*? is there such a thing as a Creator, who can *create* in you a clean heart? or is the whole thing simply evolution? Just now, and among Seventh-day Adventists, the question from this day until the end of the world must be, Do you believe in the Creator? And when you believe in the Creator, how is it that he creates?—Of course you say, it is by the word of God. Very good. Now, does he create things for *you* by his word? Are *you* a creationist for the other evolutionists, and then an evolutionist for the other creationists? How is it?

Another thing. The word says, "Be *ye* clean," He said, back yonder, "Let there be light: and there was light." He said to the leper, "Be thou clean;" and "immediately" he was clean. He says now to you, "Be ye clean," and what now? Every one of you—what do you say? [Voice: "It is so."] Then for your soul's sake put yourself upon that creative word. Recognize the creative energy in the word of God which comes to you in the Bible; for this word of God in the Bible is the same here to you to-day that it was when it spoke into space the worlds on high, and brought light out of darkness, and cleansing to the leper. That word spoken to you to-day, if received, creates you new in Christ Jesus; that word, spoken into the dark waste and void space of your heart, if received, produces there the light of God; that word spoken to-day to you, afflicted with the leprosy of sin, if received, immediately cleanses you, Let it. Let it.

How shall I be clean?—By the creative energy of that word, *"Be* ye clean." Therefore it is written, "Now *ye are* clean through the word which I have spoken unto you." John 15:3. Are you? Will you from this moment be a creationist? Or will you go on being an evolutionist?

See what a blessed thing this is. When you read the word, receive the word, and think upon the word, what is it to you all the time? O, it is creation! The creative energy is in you producing the things which the word speaks; and you are living in the very presence of the power of creation. Creation is going on in your life. God is creating, in you, righteousness, holiness, truth, faithfulness,—every good and gracious thing.

And when this is so, your Sabbath-keeping will amount to something, because the Sabbath is a memorial of creation,—the sign that he who observes it knows the Creator, and is acquainted with the process of creation. But as certainly as you are an evolutionist, your Sabbath-keeping is a fraud.

Unless you recognize the word of God day by day as a creative energy in your life, your Sabbath-keeping is a fraud; because the Sabbath is a memorial of creation. It is "a sign between me and you, that [by which] ye may *know* that I am the Lord your God," the Creator of all things.

In the second chapter of Ephesians, eighth to tenth verses, we read: "For by grace are ye saved through faith; and that not of yourselves: it is the gift of God: not of works, lest any man should boast. For we are *his* workmanship, *created* in Christ Jesus unto good works, which God hath before ordained that we should walk in them."

You need not expect to get any good works out of yourself. You have been trying. The evolutionist tries, and is always *trying*, without accomplishing it. Why go about trying to do good works, when you know you fail? Listen: there will never be any good thing in you, of any kind whatever, from now till the world's end, except it is *created there by the Creator himself, by his word*, which has in it the creative energy. Do not forget that. Do you want to walk in good works when you go out of this house? It can be done only by being created in Jesus Christ unto those good works. Stop *trying*. Look to the Creator, and receive his creative word. "Let the word of Christ dwell in you richly;" *then* those good works will appear; you will be a Christian. Then, because you live with the Creator, and are in the presence of the creative energy, you will have that pleasant, quiet peace, and genuine strength and building up, that belong to a Christian.

When he tells you that "we are his workmanship, created in Christ Jesus unto good works, which God hath before ordained that we should walk in them," then recognize the Creator,—recognize only the good works that are *created* in you, paying no attention whatever to any work that is not *created* there, because there is nothing good but what is created by the Lord.

Now you are created new in Christ Jesus. He says so. Thank him that it is so. What! will you be an evolutionist on that verse? That is the present tense, "We *are* his workmanship," we *are* created in Christ Jesus unto good works. Are you? The word is spoken. It is the creative word. How much time are you going to allow between that word of God, and your being created new? Of the creation in the beginning, you said that any man who allows even a minute to pass between the *word* and the *thing*, is an evolutionist. What are you now as to this word of God, which creates men in Christ Jesus unto good works? Are *you* an evolutionist *here?* Come, let us all be creationists.

Do you not see that *in this way* it will not require a long, tedious, wearing process to be made ready to meet the Lord in glory? So many people are looking at themselves. They know that, in the nature of things it must take them an exceedingly long time to get fully ready to meet him. If it is done by evolution, it will *never* be done. But when it is done by creation, it will be both surely and quickly done. That word I have before referred to is the word every one here may take to himself: "While so many are hovering about the mystery of faith and godliness, they could solve the matter by proclaiming abroad [by telling it out,] 'Jesus Christ is my portion forever.' "

Do you see how much we have been evolutionists? Shall we quit? Come now, let us be creationists, and be done with it. Let us be Sabbath-keepers truly. Let us believe the Lord. He speaks forgiveness. He speaks a clean heart. He speaks holiness, he creates it. Let him create it in you. Stop being an evolutionist, and let that creative word work for you, let that creative energy work in you, that which the word pronounces; and before you leave this house, God can get you ready to meet him. Indeed, in that very thing you do meet him.

And when you have thus *met* him, and *do* thus meet him *every day,* are you not then ready to meet him? Do you believe that? You believe he made *the worlds* when he *spoke,* that *light* came by his word when he *spoke, and* that the *leper* was "immediately" *cleansed* when he spoke; but with *yourself* you think considerable time must elapse between the time when the word is spoken and the fact is accomplished. O, why will you be an evolutionist? Creation, *creation,—that* is the thing.

You and I are to call people to the supper; we are to say to all people, "Come; for all things are now ready." How can I call to a man that all things are now ready, when I myself am not ready? It is a falsehood to start with. My words will not reach him: they are but an empty sound. But O, when there is in that call the creative energy of the word that has made us ready, that has cleansed us from sin, that has created us unto good works, that holds us as the sun is held in the course which God has marked out—*then* when we go forth, and say to the world lying in wickedness, "Come; for all things are now ready," *they will hear.* They will hear in the call the tones of the voice of the Good Shepherd, and will be cheered to come to him for creative energy for themselves, to make them new creatures, and prepare them for the supper to which they have been called.

This is where we are in this world's history. God's mark is being set upon the people. But remember, he will never set his mark upon one who is not cleansed from every defilement. God will not set his seal to something that is not true, that is not good. Would you ask him to set his seal to righteousness that is altogether unrighteousness?—You would not have the face to do that. You know that he is too righteous to do such a thing. Then *he* must cleanse you, so that he can put his seal to his own work. He can not put his seal to *your* work. His seal belongs only to a document which he himself has approved. Let him write his character upon your heart, and then he can set his seal there; he can write his seal of approval *upon* your heart, only when his creative word has accomplished its purpose *in* your heart.

You can see in what a Presence we are; you can see in a measure how long it would take half to exhaust such a subject as this. But, brethren, when we do stop, let us stop in the presence of *creation.* Let us be no more evolutionists. Let not a moment pass between the word of God spoken *to* you, and the accomplishment of the thing *in* you. Thus, living in the presence of creation, walking with the Creator, upheld by creative power, inspired by the creative energy—why, with a people such as that, God can move the world in a little while.

If at the beginning you thought this was a queer subject for such an occasion as to-day [it was the closing service of the week of prayer] you can now see that it is a strictly present truth. There are only the two ways. There is no halfway ground. Every man and woman in the world is either a creationist or an evolutionist. Evolution is infidelity, it is death. Creation is Christianity, it is life. Choose Creation, Christianity, and Life, that you may live. Let us be creationists only, and creationists forever. And let all the people say, Amen.

SAVING FAITH

E. J. WAGGONER—Bible Echo Aug. 1, 1890

"But the righteousness which is of faith speaketh on this wise, Say not in thine heart, Who shall ascend into heaven? (that is, to bring Christ down from above); or, Who shall descend into the deep? (that is, to bring up Christ again from the dead.) But what saith it? The word is nigh thee, even in thy mouth, and in thy heart; that is, the word of faith, which we preach: that if thou shalt confess with thy mouth the Lord Jesus, and shalt believe in thine heart that God hath raised him from the dead, thou shalt be saved." Rom. 10:6–9.

May we accept these words, especially the statement in the last verse, as literally true? Shall we not be in danger if we do? Is not something more than faith in Christ necessary to salvation? To the first of these questions we say, Yes; and to the last two we say, No; and refer to the Scriptures for corroboration. So plain a statement cannot be other than literally true, and one that can be depended on by the trembling sinner.

As an instance in proof, take the case of the jailer at Philippi. Paul and Silas, after having been inhumanely beaten, were placed in his care. Notwithstanding their lacerated backs and their manacled feet, they prayed and sang praises to God at midnight, and suddenly an earthquake shook the prison, and all the doors were opened. It was not alone the natural fear produced by feeling the earth rock beneath him, nor yet the dread of Roman justice if the prisoners in his charge should escape, that caused the jailer to tremble. But he felt in that earthquake shock a premonition of the great Judgment, concerning which the apostles had preached; and, trembling under his load of guilt, he fell down before Paul and Silas, saying, "Sirs, what must I do to be saved?" Mark well the answer; for here was a soul in sorest extremity, and what was sufficient for him must be the message to all lost ones. To the jailer's anguished appeal, Paul replied, "Believe on the Lord Jesus Christ, and thou shalt be saved." Acts 16:30, 31. This agrees exactly with the words which we quoted from Paul to the Romans.

On one occasion the Jews said unto Jesus, "What shall we do, that we might work the works of God?" Just the thing that we want to know. Mark the reply: "This is the work of God, that ye believe on him whom he hath sent." John 6:28, 29. Would that these words might be written in letters of gold, and kept continually before the eyes of every struggling Christian. The seeming paradox is cleared up. Works are necessary; yet faith is all-sufficient, because faith does the work. Faith comprehends everything, and without faith there is nothing.

The trouble is that people in general have a faulty conception of faith. They imagine that it is mere assent, and that it is only a passive thing, to which active works must be added. But faith is active, and it is not only the most substantial thing, but the only real foundation. The law is the righteousness of God (Isa. 51:6, 7), for which we are commanded to seek (Matt. 6:33); but it cannot be kept except by faith, for the only righteousness which will stand in the Judgment is "that which is through the faith of Christ, the righteousness which is of God by faith." Phil. 3:9.

Read the words of Paul in Rom. 3:31: "Do we then make void the law through faith? God forbid; yea, we establish the law." Making void the law of God by man is not abolishing it; for that is an impossibility. It is as fixed as the throne of God. No matter what men say of the law, nor how much they trample upon it and despise it, it remains the same. The only way that men can make void the law of God is to make it of none effect in their hearts, by their disobedience. Thus in Num. 30:15, a vow that has been broken is said to have been made void. So when the apostle says that we do not make void the law through faith, he means that faith and disobedience are incompatible. No matter how much the law-breaker professes faith, the fact that he is a law-breaker shows that he has no faith. But the possession of faith is shown by the establishment of the law in the heart, so that the man does not sin against God. Let no one decry faith, as of little moment.

But does not the apostle James say that faith alone cannot save a man, and that faith without works is dead? Let us look at his words a moment. Too many have with honest intent perverted them to a dead legalism. He does say that faith without works is dead, and this agrees most fully with what we have just quoted and written. For if faith without works is dead, the absence of works shows the absence of faith; for that which is dead has no existence. If a man has faith, works will necessarily appear, and the man will not boast of either one; for by faith boasting is excluded. Rom. 3:27. Boasting is done only by those who trust wholly in dead works, or whose profession of faith is a hollow mockery.

Then how about James 2:14, which says: "What doth it profit, my brethren, though a man say he hath faith, and have not works? can faith save him?" The answer necessarily implied is, of course, that it cannot. Why not?—Because he hasn't it. What doth it profit if a man *say* he has faith, if by his wicked course he shows that he has none? Must we decry the power of faith simply because it does nothing for the man who makes a false profession of it? Paul speaks of some who profess that they know God, but who deny him by their works. Titus 1:16. The man to whom James refers is one of this class. The fact that he has no good works—no fruit of the Spirit—shows that he has no faith, despite his loud profession; and so of course faith cannot save him; for faith has no power to save a man who does not possess it.

CHRIST—THE END OF THE LAW

E. J. WAGGONER—Bible Echo Feb. 15, 1892

In Rom. 10:4 we read as follows: "For Christ is the end of the law for righteousness to every one that believeth." Before showing what this text means, it may be well to briefly show what it does *not* mean. It does not mean that Christ has put an end to the law; because (1) Christ himself said concerning the law, "I am not come to destroy." Matt. 5:17. (2) The prophet said that instead of destroying it, the Lord would "Magnify the law, and make it honorable." Isa. 42:21. (3) The law was in Christ's own heart: "Then said I, Lo, I come; in the volume of the book it is written of me, I delight to do thy will, O my God; yea, thy law is within my heart." Ps. 40:7, 8. And (4) since the law is the righteousness of God, the foundation of his government, it could not by any possibility be abolished. See Luke 16:17.

The reader must know that the word "end" does not necessarily mean "termination." It is often used in the sense of design, object, or purpose. In 1 Tim. 1:5 the same writer says: "Now the end of the commandment is charity out of a pure heart, and of a good conscience, and of faith unfeigned." The word here rendered "charity" is often rendered "love," and is so rendered in this place in the New Version. In 1 John 5:3 we read: "This is the love of God, that we keep his commandments;" and Paul himself says that "love is the fulfilling of the law." Rom. 13:10. In both these texts the same word *(agapa)* is used that occurs in 1 Tim. 1:5. Therefore we say that this text means, Now the design of the commandment (or law) is that it should be kept. Everybody will recognize this as a self-evident fact.

But this is not the ultimate design of the law. In the verse following the one under consideration, Paul quotes Moses as saying of the law that "the man that doeth those things shall live by them." Christ said to the young man, "If thou wilt enter into life, keep the commandments." Matt. 19:17. Now since the design of the law was that it should be kept, or, in other words, that it should produce righteous characters, and the promise is that those who are obedient shall live, we may say that the ultimate design of the law was to give life. And in harmony with this thought are the words of Paul, that the law "was ordained to life." Rom. 7:10.

But "all have sinned and come short of the glory of God," and "the wages of sin is death." Thus it is impossible for the law to accomplish its design in making perfect characters and consequently giving life. When a man has once broken the law, no subsequent obedience can ever make his character perfect. And therefore the law which was ordained unto life, is found to be unto death. Rom. 7:10.

If we were to stop right here, with the law unable to accomplish its purpose, we should leave all the world under condemnation and sentence of death. Now we shall see that Christ enables man to secure both righteousness and life. We read that we are "justified freely by his grace through the redemption that is in Christ Jesus." Rom. 3:24. "Therefore being justified by faith, we have peace with God through our Lord Jesus Christ." Rom. 5:1.

More than this, he enables us to keep the law. "For he [God] hath made him [Christ] to be sin for us, who knew no sin; that we might be made the righteousness of God in him." 2 Cor. 5:21. In Christ, therefore, it is possible for us to be made perfect,—the righteousness of God,—and that is just what we would have been by constant and unvarying obedience to the law.

Again we read: "There is therefore now no condemnation to them which are in Christ Jesus, who walk not after the flesh, but after the Spirit.... For what the law could not do, in that it was weak through the flesh, God, sending his own Son in the likeness of sinful flesh, and for sin, condemned sin in the flesh; that the righteousness of the law might be fulfilled in us, who walk not after the flesh, but after the Spirit." Rom. 8:1–4.

What could not the law do?—It could not free a single guilty soul from condemnation. Why not?—Because it was "weak through the flesh." There is no element of weakness in the law; the weakness is in the flesh. It is not the fault of a good tool that it cannot make a sound pillar out of a rotten stick. The law could not cleanse a man's past record, and make him sinless; and poor, fallen man had no strength resting in his flesh to enable him to keep the law. And so God imputes to believers the righteousness of Christ, who was made in the likeness of sinful flesh, so that "the righteousness of the law" might be fulfilled in their lives. And thus Christ is the end of the law.

To conclude, then, we have found that the design of the law was that it should give life because of obedience. All men have sinned, and been sentenced to death. But Christ took upon himself man's nature, and will impart of his own righteousness to those who accept his sacrifice, and finally, when they stand, through him, as doers of the law, he will fulfill to them its ultimate object, by crowning them with eternal life. And so we repeat, what we cannot too fully appreciate, that Christ is made unto us "wisdom, and righteousness, and sanctification, and redemption."

THE UNCONQUERABLE LIFE

E. J. WAGGONER—Bible Echo Oct. 15, 1892

"In Him was life, and the life was the light of men. And the light shineth in the darkness, and the darkness apprehended it not." John 1:4,5 R.V. The marginal rendering, "overcame," gives us the exact meaning of the text, and conveys a message of great comfort to the believer. Let us see what it is.

Christ is the light of the world. See John 8:12. But his light is his life, as the text quoted states. He says, "I am the light of the world; he that followeth Me shall not walk in darkness, but shall have the light of life." The whole world was in the darkness of sin. This darkness was due to lack of knowledge of God; as the apostle Paul says that the Gentiles are "darkened in their understanding, alienated from the life of God because of the ignorance that is in them because of the hardening of their heart." Eph. 4:18, R.V.

Satan, the ruler of the darkness of this world, had done his utmost to deceive men as to the true character of God. He had made the world believe that God was like men—cruel, vindictive, and passionate. Even the Jews, the people whom God had chosen to be the bearers of his light to the world, had departed from God, and while professedly separate from the heathen, were enveloped in heathen darkness. Then Christ came, and "The people which sat in darkness saw a great light, and to them which sat in the region and shadow of death, to them did light spring up." Matt. 4:16, R.V. His name was Emanuel, God with us. "God was in Christ." God refuted the falsehoods of Satan, not by loud arguments, but simply by living his life among men, so that all might see it. He demonstrated the power of the life of God, and the possibility of its being manifested in men.

The life which Christ lived was untainted by sin. Satan exerted all his powerful arts, yet he could not affect that spotless life. Its light always shone with unwavering brilliancy. Because Satan could not produce the least shadow of sin in the life, he could not bring it within his power, that of the grave. No one could take Christ's life from Him; He voluntarily laid it down. And for the same reason, when He had laid it down, Satan could not prevent Him from taking it up again. Said He, "I lay down my life that I might take it again. No man taketh it from Me, but I lay it down of myself. I have power to lay it down, and I have power to take it again. This commandment have I received of my Father." John 10:17, 18. To the same intent are the words of the apostle Peter concerning Christ: "Whom God hath raised up having loosed the pains of death; because it was not possible that He should be holden of it." Acts 2:24. Thus was demonstrated the right of the Lord Jesus Christ to be made a high priest "after the power of an endless life." Heb. 7:16.

This endless, spotless life Christ gives to all who believe on Him. "As Thou hast given Him power over all flesh, that He should give eternal life to as many as Thou hast given Him. And this is life eternal, that they might know Thee, the only true God, and Jesus Christ, whom Thou hast sent." John 17:2, 3. Christ dwells in the hearts of all those who believe on Him. "I am crucified with Christ; nevertheless I live; yet not I, but Christ liveth in me; and the life which I now live in the flesh I live by the faith of the Son of God, who loved me, and gave Himself for me." Gal. 2–20. See also Eph. 3:16, 17.

Christ, the light of the world, dwelling in the hearts of his followers, constitutes them the light of the world. Their light comes not from themselves, but from Christ, who dwells in them. Their life is not from themselves; but it is the life of Christ manifest in their mortal flesh. See 2 Cor. 4:11. This is what it is to live "a Christian life."

This living light comes from God in a never-failing stream. The psalmist exclaims: "For with Thee is the fountain of life, in thy light shall we see light." Ps. 36:9. "And He showed me a pure river of water of life, clear as crystal, proceeding out of the throne of God and of the Lamb." Rev. 22:1. "And the Spirit and the Bride say, Come. And let him that heareth say, Come. And let him that is athirst, come. And whosoever will, let him take the water of life freely." Rev. 2:17.

"Jesus said unto them, Verily, verily, I say unto you, Except ye eat the flesh of the Son of man, and drink his blood, ye have no life in you. Whoso eateth my flesh, and drinketh my blood, hath eternal life; and I will raise him up at the last day." John 6:53, 54. This life of Christ we eat and drink by feasting upon his Word, for He added, "It is the spirit that quickeneth; the flesh profiteth nothing; the words that I speak unto you, they are spirit, and they are life." Verse 63. Christ dwells in his inspired Word, and through it we get his life. This life is given freely to all who will receive it, as we read above; and again we read that Jesus stood and cried, saying, "If any man thirst, let him come unto Me and drink." John 7:37.

This life is the Christian's light, and it is that which makes him a light to others. It is his life; and the blessed comfort to him is that no matter how great the darkness through which he has to pass, no darkness has power to put out that light. That light of life is his as long as he exercises faith, and the darkness cannot affect it. Let all, therefore, who profess the name of the Lord, have the confidence that can say, "Rejoice not against me, O mine enemy; when I fall, I shall arise; when I sit in darkness, the Lord shall be a light unto me." Micah 7:8.

FAITH

E. J. WAGGONER—Bible Echo Aug. 17, 1896

"Whatsoever is not of faith is sin." Rom. 14:23.

Therefore it is that "being justified"—made righteous—"by faith, we have peace with God through our Lord Jesus Christ." Rom. 5:1.

Faith, not works, is that through which men are saved. "For by grace are ye saved through faith; and that not of yourselves; it is the gift of God; not of works, lest any man should boast." Eph. 2:8, 9.

"Where is boasting, then? It is excluded. By what law? of works? Nay: but by the law of faith. Therefore we conclude that a man is justified by faith without the deeds of the law." Rom. 3:27, 28.

The gospel excludes boasting, and boasting is a natural consequence of all attempts at justification by works; yet the gospel does not exclude works. On the contrary, works—good works—are the one grand object of the gospel. "For we are His workmanship, created in Christ Jesus unto good works, which God hath before prepared that we should walk in them." Eph. 2:10, with margin.

There is not the slightest contradiction here. The difference is between our works and God's works. Our works are always faulty; God's works are always perfect; therefore it is God's works that we need in order to be perfect. But we are not able to do God's works, for He is infinite, and we are nothing. For a man to think himself able to do God's works is the highest presumption. We laugh when a five-year-old boy imagines that he can do his father's work; how much more foolish for puny man to imagine that he can do the works of the Almighty.

Goodness is not an abstract thing; it is action, and action is found only in living beings. And since God alone is good, only His works are of any account. Only the man who has God's works is righteous. But since no man can do God's works, it necessarily follows that God must give them to us, if we are saved. This is just what He does for all who believe.

When the Jews in their self-sufficiency asked, "What shall we do that we might work the works of God?" Jesus replied, "This is the work of God, that ye believe on Him whom He hath sent." John 6:28, 29. Faith works. Gal. 5:6; 1 Thess. 1:3. It brings God's works into the believing one, since it brings Christ into the heart (Eph. 3:17), and in Him is all the fullness of God. Col. 2:9. Jesus Christ is "the same yesterday, and to-day, and forever" (Heb. 13:8), and therefore God not only *was* but *is* in Christ, reconciling the world unto Himself. So if Christ dwells in the heart by faith, the works of God will be manifest in the life; "for it is God which worketh in you both to will and to do of His good pleasure." Phil. 2:13.

How this is done, is not within the range of our comprehension. We do not need to know how it is done, since we do not have it to do. The fact is enough for us. We can no more understand how God does His works, than we can do those works. So the Christian life is always a mystery, even to the Christian himself. It is a life hidden with Christ in God. Col. 3:3. It is hidden even from the Christian's own sight. Christ in man, the hope of glory, is the mystery of the gospel. Col. 1:27.

In Christ we are created unto good works which God has already prepared for us. We have only to accept them by faith. The acceptance of those good works is the acceptance of Christ. How long "before" did God prepare those good works for us?—"The works were finished from the foundation of the world. For He spake in a certain place of the seventh day on this wise, And God did rest the seventh day from all His works. And in this place again, If they shall"—*i.e.*, they, the unbelieving, shall not—"enter into My rest." Heb. 4:3–5. But "we which have believed do enter into rest."

The Sabbath, therefore,—the seventh day of the week—is God's rest. God gave the Sabbath as a sign by which men might know that He is God, and that He sanctifies. Eze. 20:12, 20. Sabbath-keeping has nothing whatever to do with justification by works, but is, on the contrary, the sign and seal of justification by faith; it is a sign that man gives up his own sinful works and accepts God's perfect works. Since the Sabbath is not a work, but a rest, it is the mark of rest in God through faith in our Lord Jesus Christ.

No other day than the seventh day of the week can stand as the mark of perfect rest in God, because on that day alone did God rest from all His works. It is the rest of the seventh day, into which He says the unbelieving cannot enter. It alone of all the days of the week is the rest day, and it is inseparably connected with God's perfect work.

On the other six days, including the first day of the week, God worked. On those days we also may and ought to work. Yet on every one of them we also may and ought to rest in God. This will be the case if our works are "wrought in God." John 3:21. So men should rest in God every day in the week; but the seventh day alone can be the sign of that rest.

Two things may be noted as self-evident conclusions of the truths already set forth. One is that the setting apart of another day than the seventh, as a sign of acceptance of Christ and of rest in God through Him, is in reality a sign of rejection of Him. Since it is the substitution of man's way for God's way, it is in reality the sign of man's assumption of superiority above God, and of the idea that man can save himself by his own works. Not every one who observes another day has that assumption, by any means. There are many who love the Lord in sincerity and who accept Him in humility, who observe another day than that which God has given as the sign of rest in Him. They simply have not learned the full and proper expression of faith. But their sincerity, and the fact that God accepts their unfeigned faith, does not alter the fact that the day which they observe is the sign of exaltation above God. When such hear God's gracious warning they will forsake the sign of apostasy as they would a plague-stricken house.

The other point is that people cannot be forced to keep the Sabbath, inasmuch as it is a sign of faith, and no man can be forced to believe. Faith comes spontaneously as the result of hearing God's word. No man can even force himself to believe, much less can he compel somebody else. By force a man's fears may be so wrought upon that he may say he believes, and he may act as though he believed. That is to say, a man who fears man rather than God may be forced to lie. But "no lie is of the truth." Therefore since the Sabbath is the sign of perfect faith, it is the sign of perfect liberty—"the glorious liberty of the children of God"—the liberty which the Spirit gives; for the Sabbath, as a part of God's law, is spiritual. And so, finally, let no one deceive himself with the thought that an outward observance of even God's appointed rest-day—the seventh day—without faith and trust in God's word alone, is the keeping of God's Sabbath. "For whatsoever is not of faith is sin."

BOUNDLESS GRACE—FREE TO ALL

A. T. JONES—RH April 17, 1894

"Unto every one of us is given grace according to the measure of the gift of Christ." Eph. 4:7. The measure of the gift of Christ is "all the fullness of the Godhead bodily." This is true whether viewed as the measure of the gift which God made in giving Christ, or as the measure of the gift which Christ himself gave. For the gift that God gave is his only begotten Son, and in "him dwelleth all the fullness of the Godhead bodily." Therefore, from this standpoint, the measure of the gift of Christ being only the measure of the fullness of the Godhead bodily, and this being only the measure of the grace that is given to every one of us, it follows that unto every one of us is given grace without measure, simply boundless grace.

Viewed from the measure of the gift in which Christ himself gives to us, it is the same; because "he gave himself for us;" he gave himself for our sins, and in this he gave himself *to* us. And as in him dwelleth all the fullness of the Godhead bodily, and as he gave himself, then the measure of the gift of Christ on his own part is also only the measure of the fullness of the Godhead bodily. It therefore follows that from this standpoint also, the measure of grace that is given to every one of us is only the measure of the fullness of the Godhead, that is, simply immeasurable.

Thus in whatever way it is viewed, the plain word of the Lord is that unto every one of us he has given grace to the measure of the fullness of the Godhead bodily; that is, boundless, immeasurable grace—all the grace he has. This is good. But it is just the Lord, it is just like the Lord to do that; for he is good.

And this boundless grace is all given, given freely, to "*every one* of us." To *us* it is. To you and me, just as we are. And that is good. We need just that much grace to make us what the Lord wants us to be. And he is just so kind as to give it all to us freely, that we may be indeed just what he wants us to be.

The Lord wants every one of us to be saved, and that with the very fullness of salvation. And therefore he has given to every one of us the very fullness of grace, because it is grace that brings the salvation. For it is written, "The grace of God *that bringeth salvation* hath appeared to all men." Titus 2:11. Thus the Lord wants all to be saved, and therefore he gave all of his grace, bringing salvation to all. The marginal reading of this text tells it that way, and it is just as true as the reading in the verse itself. Here it is: "The grace of God that bringeth salvation to all men, hath appeared." All the grace of God is given freely to every one, bringing salvation to all. Whether all or any one will receive it, that is another question. What we are studying now is the truth and the fact that God *has given* it. Having given it all, he is clear, even though men may reject it,

The Lord wants us to be perfect: and so it is written: "Be ye therefore perfect, even as your Father which is in heaven is perfect." Desiring that we shall be perfect, he has given us, every one, all the grace that he has, bringing the fullness of his salvation, that every man may be presented perfect in Christ Jesus. The very purpose of this gift of his boundless grace is that we may be made *like Jesus,* who is the image of God. Even so it is written: "Unto every one of us is given grace according to the measure of the gift of Christ,…*for the perfecting* of the saints;…till *we all* come in the unity of the faith, and of the knowledge of the Son of God, unto *a perfect man,* unto the *measure* of the stature of *the fullness of* Christ."

Do you want to be like Jesus? Then receive the grace that he has so fully and so freely given. Receive it in the measure in which *he has given it,* not in the measure in which you think you deserve it. Yield yourself to it, that it may work in you and for you the wondrous purpose for which it is given, and it will do it. It will make you like Jesus. It will accomplish the purpose and the wish of him who has given it. "Yield yourselves unto God." "I beseech you also that ye receive not the grace of God in vain."

SHALL IT BE GRACE OR SIN?

A. T. JONES—RH Sept. 1, 1896

It can never be repeated too often, that under the reign of grace it is just as easy to do right, as under the reign of sin it is easy to do wrong. This must be so; for if there is not more power in grace than there is in sin, then there can be no salvation from sin. But there is salvation from sin; this no one who believes Christianity can deny.

Yet salvation from sin certainly depends upon there being more power in grace than there is in sin. Then, there being more power in grace than there is in sin, it cannot possibly be otherwise than that wherever the power of grace can have control, it will be just as easy to do right as without this it is easy to do wrong.

No man ever yet naturally found it difficult to do wrong. His great difficulty has always been to do right. But this is because man naturally is enslaved to a power—the power of sin that is absolute in its reign. And so long as that power has sway, it is not only difficult but impossible to do the good that he knows and that he would. But let a mightier power than that have sway, then is it not plain enough that it will be just as easy to serve the will of the mightier power, when it reigns, as it was to serve the will of the other power when it reigned?

But grace is not simply more powerful than is sin. If this were indeed all, even then there would be fullness of hope and good cheer to every sinner in the world. But this, good as it would be, is not all; it is not nearly all. There is much more power in grace than there is in sin. For "where sin abounded, grace did much more abound." And just as much more power in grace than there is in sin, just so much more hope and good cheer there are for every sinner in the world.

How much more power, then, is there in grace than there is in sin? Let me think a moment. Let me ask myself a question or two. Whence comes grace?—From God, to be sure. "Grace be unto you, and peace, from God our Father, and from the Lord Jesus Christ." Whence comes sin?—From the devil, of course. Sin is of the devil; for the devil sinneth from the beginning. Well, then, how much more power is there in grace than there is in sin? It is as plain as A B C that there is just as much more power in grace than there is in sin, as there is more power in God than there is in the devil. It is therefore also perfectly plain that the reign of grace is the reign of God; and that the reign of sin is the reign of Satan. And is it not therefore perfectly plain also, that it is just as easy to serve God by the power of God as it is to serve Satan with the power of Satan?

Where the difficulty comes in, in all this, is that so many people try to serve God with the power of Satan. But that can never be done. "Either make the tree good, and his fruit good; or else make the tree corrupt, and his fruit corrupt." Men cannot gather grapes of thorns, nor figs of thistles. The tree must be made good, root and branch. It must be made new. "Ye must be born again." "In Christ Jesus neither circumcision availeth anything, nor uncircumcision, but a new creature." Let no one ever attempt to serve God with anything but the present, living power of God, that makes him a new creature; with nothing but the much more abundant grace that condemns sin in the flesh, and reigns through righteousness unto eternal life by Jesus Christ our Lord. Then the service of God will indeed be in "newness of life;" then it will be found that his yoke is indeed "easy" and his burden "light;" then his service will be found indeed to be with "joy unspeakable and full of glory."

Did Jesus ever find it difficult to do right? Every one will instantly say, No. But why? he was just as human as we are. He took flesh and blood the same as ours. "The Word was made flesh, and dwelt among us." And the kind of flesh that he was made in this world, was precisely such as was in this world. "In all things it behooved him to be made like unto his brethren." "In all things!" It does not say, In all things *but one*. There is no exception. He was made in all things like as we are. He was of himself as weak as we are; for he said, "I can of mine own self do nothing."

Why, then, being in all things like as we are, did he find it always easy to do right?—Because he never trusted to himself, but his trust was always in God alone. All his dependence was upon the grace of God. He always sought to serve God, only with the power of God. And therefore the Father dwelt in him, and did the works of righteousness. Therefore it was always easy for him to do right. But as he is, so are we in this world. He has left us an example, that we should follow his steps. "It is God which worketh in *you* both to will and to do of his good pleasure," as well as in him. All power in heaven and in earth is given unto him; and he desires that you may be strengthened with *all might,* according to his glorious power. "In him dwelleth all the fullness of the Godhead bodily;" and he strengthens you with might by his Spirit in the inner man, that Christ may dwell in your heart by faith, that *you* may be "filled with all the fullness of God."

True, Christ partook of the divine nature, and so do you if you are a child of promise, and not of the flesh; for by the promises ye are partakers of the divine nature. There was nothing given to him in this world, and he had nothing in this world, that is not freely given to you, or that you may not have.

All this is in order that you may walk in newness of life; that henceforth you may not serve sin; that you may be the servant of righteousness only; that you may be freed from sin; that sin may not have dominion over you; that you may glorify God on the earth; and that you may be like Jesus. And therefore "unto every one of us is given grace according to the measure of the gift of Christ.... Till we all come in the unity of the faith, and the knowledge of the Son of God, unto a perfect man, unto the measure of the stature of the fullness of Christ." And I "beseech you also that ye receive not the grace of God in vain."

RECEIVE NOT THE GRACE OF GOD IN VAIN

A. T. JONES—RH Sept. 22, 1896

Can every believer have grace enough to keep him free from sinning?—Yes. Indeed, everybody in the world can have enough to keep him from sinning. Enough is given; and it is given for this purpose. If any one does not have it, it is not because enough has not been given; but because he does not take that which has been given. For "unto every one of us is given grace according to the measure of the gift of Christ." Eph. 4:7. The measure of the gift of Christ is himself wholly, and that is the measure of "all the fullness of the Godhead bodily." To the fullness of the Godhead there is, indeed, no measure; it is boundless, it is simply the infinity of God. Yet that is the only measure of the grace that is given to every one of us. The boundless measure of the fullness of the Godhead is the only thing that can express the proportion of grace that is given to every one who is in this world. For "where sin abounded, grace did much more abound." This grace is given in order that "as sin hath reigned unto death, even so might grace reign through righteousness unto eternal life by Jesus Christ our Lord," and in order that sin shall not have dominion over you, because you are under grace.

It is given also "for the perfecting of the saints." The object of it is to bring each one to perfection in Christ Jesus to the perfection too, that is fully up to God's standard; for it is given for the building up of the body of Christ, "till we all come in the unity of the faith, and of the knowledge of the Son of God, unto a perfect man, unto the measure of the stature of the fullness of Christ." It is given to "every one of us," "till we all come" to perfection, even by the measure of the stature of the fullness of Christ. Again, this grace is given to every one where sin abounds; and it brings salvation to every one to whom it is given. Bringing salvation in itself, the measure of the salvation which it brings to every one is only the measure of its own fullness, which is nothing less than the measure of the fullness of the Godhead.

As boundless grace is given to every one bringing salvation to the extent of its own full measure, then if any one does not have boundless salvation, why is it?—Plainly it can be only because he will not take that which is given.

As boundless grace is given to every one, in order that it shall reign in him against all the power of sin, as certainly as ever sin reigned; and in order that sin shall not have dominion, then if sin still reigns in any one, if sin yet has dominion over any one, where lies the fault?—Clearly it lies only in this, that he will not allow the grace to do for him and in him that which it is given to do. By unbelief he frustrates the grace of God. So far as he is concerned, the grace has been given in vain.

But every believer, by his very profession, says that he has received the grace of God. Then if in the believer grace does not reign instead of sin; if grace does not have dominion instead of sin, it is plain enough that he is receiving the grace of God in vain. If grace is not bringing the believer onward toward a perfect man in the measure of the stature of the fullness of Christ, then he is receiving the grace of God in vain. Therefore the exhortation of the Scripture is, "We then, as workers together with him, beseech you also that ye receive not the grace of God in vain." 2 Cor. 6:1.

The grace of God is fully able to accomplish that for which it is given, if only it is allowed to work. We have seen that grace being altogether from God, the power of grace is nothing but the power of God. It is plain enough therefore that the power of God is abundantly able to accomplish all for which it is given,—the salvation of the soul, deliverance from sin and from the power of it, the reign of righteousness in the life, and the perfecting of the believer unto the measure of the stature of the fullness of Christ,—if only it can have place in the heart and in the life to work according to the will of God. But the power of God is "unto salvation to every one that *believeth.*" Unbelief frustrates the grace of God. Many believe and receive the grace of God for the salvation from sins that are past, but are content with that, and do not give it the same place in the soul, to reign against the power of sin, that they did to save from sins of the past. This, too, is but another phase of unbelief. So as to the one great final object of grace—the perfection of the life in the likeness of Christ—they do practically receive the grace of God in vain.

"We then, as workers together with him, beseech you also that ye receive not the grace of God in vain. (For he saith, I have heard thee in a time accepted, and in the day of salivation have I succored thee: behold, *now* is the accepted time, behold, *now* is the day of salvation.) Giving no offense in anything, that the ministry be not blamed." Nor does this word "ministry" refer simply to the ordained ministry of the pulpit; it includes every one who receives the grace of God, or that has named the name of Christ. For "as every man hath received the gift, even so minister the same one to another, as good stewards of the manifold grace of God." Therefore he does not want any one to receive the grace of God in vain, lest that grace and its blessed working be misrepresented to the world, and so men be further hindered from yielding to it. He does not want his grace to be received in vain, because when it is, offense is given in many things, and the ministry of grace itself is blamed. Yet when the grace of God is not received in vain, but is given the place that belongs to it, "no offense" will be given "in anything," and the ministry will not only be not blamed but will be blest.

And now to show how complete and all-pervading the reign of grace will be in the life where it is not received in vain, the Lord has set down the following list, embracing "all things," and in which we shall approve ourselves unto God. Read it carefully:—

"In all things approving ourselves" unto God,
"In much patience,
In afflictions,
In necessities,
In distresses,
In stripes,
In imprisonments,

In tumults,
In labors,
In watchings,
In fastings;
By pureness,
By knowledge,
By long-suffering,
By kindness,
By the Holy Ghost,
By love unfeigned,
By the word of truth,
By the power of God,
By the armor of righteousness on the right hand and on the left,
By honor and dishonor,
By evil report and good report:
As deceivers, and yet true;
As unknown, and yet well known;
As dying, and, behold, we live;
As chastened, and not killed;
As sorrowful, yet always rejoicing;
As poor, yet making many rich;
As having nothing, and yet possessing all things."

This list covers all the experiences that can ever enter into the life of any believer in this world. It shows that where the grace of God is not received in vain, that grace will so take possession and control of the life, that every experience that enters into the life will be taken by grace, and turned to making us approved unto God, and building us up in perfection unto the measure of the stature of the fullness of Christ. "We then, as workers together with him, beseech you also that ye receive not the grace of God in vain."

SINFUL FLESH

A. T. JONES—RH Apr. 18, 1899

There is a serious and very bothersome mistake, which is made by many persons.

That mistake is made in thinking that when they are converted, their old sinful flesh is blotted out.

In other words, they make the mistake of thinking that they are to be delivered from the flesh by having it taken away from them altogether.

Then, when they find that this is not so, when they find that the same old flesh, with its inclinations, its besetments, and its enticements, is still there, they are not prepared for it, and so become discouraged, and are ready to think that they never were converted at all.

And yet, if they would think a little, they ought to be able to see that that *is* all a mistake. Did you not have exactly the same body after you were converted that you had before? Was not that body composed of exactly the same material—the same flesh and bones and blood—after you were converted as that of which it was composed before? To these questions everybody will promptly say Yes. And plainly that is the truth.

And now there are further questions: Was not that flesh also of exactly the same *quality* as before? Was it not still human flesh, natural flesh, as certainly as it was before?—To this also everybody will say Yes.

Then also a still further question: It being the same flesh, and of the same quality,—it still being human flesh, natural flesh,—is it not also still just as certainly *sinful* flesh as it was before?

Just here is where creeps in the mistake of these many persons. To this last question they are inclined to think that the answer should be "No," when it must be only a decided "Yes." And this decided "Yes" must be maintained so long as we continue in this natural body.

And when it is decided and constantly maintained that the flesh of the converted person is still sinful flesh, and only sinful flesh, he is so thoroughly convinced that in his flesh dwells no good thing that he will never allow a shadow of confidence in the flesh. And this being so, his sole dependence is upon something other than the flesh, even upon the Holy Spirit of God; his source of strength and hope is altogether exclusive of the flesh, even in Jesus Christ only. And being everlastingly watchful, suspicious, and thoroughly distrustful of the flesh, he never can expect any good thing from that source, and so is prepared by the power of God to beat back and crush down without mercy every impulse or suggestion that may arise from it; and so does not fail, does not become discouraged, but goes on from victory to victory and from strength to strength.

Conversion, then, you see, does not put new flesh upon the old spirit; but a new Spirit within the old flesh. It does not propose to bring new flesh to the old mind, but a new mind to the old flesh. Deliverance and victory are not gained by having the human nature taken away; but by receiving *the divine nature* to subdue and have dominion over the human,—not by the taking away of the sinful flesh, but by the sending in of the *sinless Spirit* to conquer and condemn sin in the flesh.

The Scripture does not say, Let this *flesh* be upon you, which was also upon Christ; but it *does* say, "Let this *mind* be in you, which was also in Christ Jesus." Phil. 2:5.

The Scripture does not say, Be ye transformed by the renewing of your *flesh;* but it does say, "Be ye transformed by the renewing of your *mind.*" Rom, 12:2. We shall be trans*lated* by the renewing of our *flesh;* but we must be trans*formed* by the renewing of our *minds.*

The Lord Jesus took the same flesh and blood, the same human nature, that we have,—flesh just like our sinful flesh,—and because of sin, and by the power of the Spirit of God through the divine mind that was in him, "condemned sin in the flesh." Rom. 8:3. And therein is our deliverance (Rom. 7:25), therein is our victory. "Let this mind be in you, which was also in Christ Jesus." "A new heart will I give you, and a new Spirit will I put within you."

Do not be discouraged at sight of sinfulness in the flesh. It is only in the light of the Spirit of God, and by the discernment of the mind of Christ, that you can see so much sinfulness in your flesh; and the more sinfulness you see in your flesh, the more of the Spirit of God you certainly have. This is a sure test. Then when you see sinfulness abundant in you, thank the Lord that you have so much of the Spirit of God that you can see so much of the sinfulness; and know of a surety that when sinfulness abounds, grace much more abounds in order that "as sin hath reigned unto death, even so might grace reign through righteousness unto eternal life by Jesus Christ our Lord."

A DEAD FORMALISM–I

A. T. JONES—Bible Echo Jan. 28, 1895

Unbelieving Israel, not having the righteousness which is of faith, and so not appreciating the great sacrifice that the Heavenly Father has made, sought righteousness by virtue *of the offering itself,* and because of the merit of presenting the offering.

Thus was perverted every form of service, and everything which God had appointed to be the means of expression to a living faith, and which could not have any real meaning except by the living presence and power of Christ Himself in the life. And even this was not enough. For, not finding the peace and satisfaction of an accomplished righteousness in any of this, nor in all of it together, they heaped upon these things which the Lord had appointed for another purpose, but which they had perverted to purposes of their own invention,—they heaped upon these things ten thousand traditions, exactions, and hair-splitting distinctions of their own invention; and all, *all,* in a vain hope of attaining to righteousness. For the rabbis taught what was practically a confession of despair, that "if but one person could only for one day keep the whole law and not offend in one point— nay, if but one person could but keep that one point of the law which affected the due observance of the Sabbath—then the troubles of Israel would be ended, and the Messiah at last would come."—Farrar, "Life and Work of St. Paul," p.37. See also pp. 36, 83. What could possibly more fittingly describe a dead formalism than does this? And yet for all this conscious dearth in their own lives, there was still enough supposed merit to cause them to count themselves so much better than other people that all others were but as dogs in comparison.

It is not so with those who are accounted righteous by the Lord upon a living faith freely exercised. For when the Lord counts a man righteous, he is actually righteous before God, and by this very fact is separated from all the people of the world. But this is not because of any excellence of his own, nor of the "merit" of anything that he has done. It is altogether because of the excellence of the Lord and of what *He* has done. And the man for whom this has been done, knows that in himself he is no better than anybody else; but rather in the light of the righteousness of God that is freely imparted to him, he, in the humility of true faith, willingly counts others better than himself. Phil. 2:3.

This giving themselves great credit for what they themselves had done, and counting themselves better than all other people upon the merit of what they had done—this were at once to land men fully in the complete self-righteousness of Phariseeism. They counted themselves so much better than all other people that there could not possibly be any basis of comparison. It seemed to them a perfectly ruinous revolution to preach as the truth of God that "there is no respect of persons with God."

And what of the actual life of such people, all this time? O, it was only a life of injustice and oppression, malice and envy, variance and emulation, backbiting and tale bearing, hypocrisy and meanness; boasting of their great honour of the law, and through breaking the law dishonouring God: their hearts filled with murder, and their tongues crying loudly for the blood of One of their brethren, yet they could not cross the threshold of a Roman tribunal "lest they should be defiled!" Intense sticklers for the Sabbath, yet spending the holy day in spying treachery and conspiracy to murder.

What God thought and still thinks of all such ways as this, is shown plainly enough for our present purpose, in just two short passages of scripture. Here is His word to Israel—the ten tribes—while yet their day lingered:—

"I hate, I despise your feast days, and I will not smell in your solemn assemblies. Though ye offer Me burnt-offerings and your meat-offerings, I will not accept them; neither will I regard the peace-offerings of your fat beasts. Take thou away from Me the noise of thy songs; for I will not hear the melody of thy viols. But let judgment run down as waters, and righteousness as a mighty stream." Amos 5:21–24.

And to Judah near the same time He said the same thing, in these words:

"Hear the word of the Lord, ye rulers of Sodom; give ear unto the law of our God, ye people of Gomorrah. To what purpose is the multitude of your sacrifices unto Me? saith the Lord: I am full of the burnt-offerings of rams, and the fat of fed beasts; and I delight not in the blood of bullocks, or of lambs, or of he-goats. When ye come to appear before Me, who hath required this at your hand, to tread My courts? Bring no more vain oblations; incense is an abomination unto Me; the new moons and sabbaths, the calling of assemblies, I cannot away with; it is iniquity, even the solemn meeting. Your new moons and your appointed feasts My soul hateth: they are a trouble unto Me; I am weary to bear them. And when ye spread forth your hands, I will hide Mine eyes from you; yea, when ye make many prayers, I will not hear; your hands are full of blood.

"Wash ye, make you clean; put away the evil of your doings from before Mine eyes; cease to do evil; learn to do well; seek judgment, relieve the oppressed, judge the fatherless, plead for the widow. Come now, and let us reason together, saith the Lord: though your sins be as scarlet, they shall be as white as snow; though they be red like crimson, they shall be as wool." Isa. 1:10–18.

The Lord Himself had appointed these feast days and solemn assemblies, these burnt-offerings, meat-offerings, and peace-offerings; but now He says He hates them and will not accept them. Their fine songs, sung by their trained choirs, and accompanied with instruments of music, making a grand display—all this that they got off for wonderfully fine *music,* He called *"noise,"* and wanted it taken away.

He had never appointed any feast days, nor solemn assemblies, nor sacrifices, nor offerings, nor songs, for any such purpose as that for which these were being used. He had appointed all these as the means of worshipful expression of a living faith by which the Lord Himself should abide in the heart and work righteousness in the life, so that in righteousness they *could* judge the fatherless and plead for the widow; and so that judgment *could* run down as waters, and righteousness as a mighty stream.

Songs sung in the pomp and stylish intonation of a vain show, are but *"noise;"* while the simple expression, "Our Father," flowing from a heart touched by the power of a true and living faith and "spoken in sincerity by human lips, is music" which enters into the inclining ear (Ps. 116:2) of the Heavenly Father, and brings divine blessing in power to the soul.

This and this alone is what He had appointed these things for; and never, never to be used in the hollow pretense of a dead formalism to answer in righteousness for the iniquity of a carnal heart. Nothing but the washing away of the sins by the blood of the Lamb of God, and the purifying of the heart by living faith—nothing but this could ever make these things acceptable to Him who appointed them.

A DEAD FORMALISM–II

A. T. JONES—Bible Echo Feb. 4, 1895

EVEN this side of the cross of Christ, which itself should be the everlasting destruction of it, the same dead formalism, an empty profession, has exalted itself, and has been the bane of the profession of Christianity everywhere. Very soon, unconverted men crept into the church and exalted themselves in the place of Christ. Not finding the living presence of Christ in the heart by living faith, they have ever since sought to have the forms of Christianity supply the lack of His presence, which alone can give meaning and life to these forms.

In this system of perverseness, regeneration is through the form of baptism, and even this by a mere sprinkling of a few drops of water; the real presence of Christ is in the form of the Lord's supper; the hope of salvation is in being connected with a form of the church. And so on throughout the whole list of the forms of Christianity. Not content with thus perverting the divinely appointed forms of Christianity, they have heaped upon this, ten thousand inventions of their own, in penances, pilgrimages, traditions, and hair-splitting distinctions.

And, as of old, and always with mere formalists, the life is simply and continually the manifestation of the works of the flesh,—strife and contention; hypocrisy and iniquity; persecution, spying, treachery, and every evil work. *This is the Papacy.*

This evil spirit of a dead formalism, however, has spread itself far beyond the bounds of the organized Papacy. It is the bane of the profession of Christianity everywhere to-day; and even the profession of the Christianity of the third angel's message has not entirely escaped it. It is to be the world-wide prevailing evil of the last days up to the very coming of the Lord in glory in the Clouds of heaven.

For, "this know also, that in the last days perilous times shall come. For men shall be lovers of their own selves, covetous, boasters, proud, blasphemers, disobedient to parents, unthankful, unholy, without natural affection, truce-breakers, false accusers, incontinent, fierce, despisers of those that are good, traitors, heady, high-minded, lovers of pleasures more than lovers of God, *having a form godliness, but denying the power thereof:* from such turn away." 2 Tim. 3:1–5.

This all-prevailing form of godliness without the power, and which even denies the power, is the dead formalism against which we are to fight the good fight of living faith. The living faith which is brought to the world in the third angel's message is to save us from being swallowed up in this worldwide sea of a dead formalism,

How is it with you individually to-day? Is yours a dead formalism, or a living faith? Have you the form of godliness without the power? or have you by living faith the living presence and power of the living Saviour in the heart, giving divine meaning, life, and joy to all the forms of worship and of service which Christ has appointed; and working the works of God and manifesting the fruits of the Spirit in all the life?

Except as the means of finding Christ the living Saviour *in the word,* and the living faith of Him, even this word itself can be turned to a dead formalism now as it was of old when He was on the earth. He said to them then (Revised Version), "Ye search the Scriptures, because *ye think that in them we have eternal life;* and these are they which bear witness of Me. And ye will not *come to Me that ye may have life."* John 5:39, 40.

They thought to find eternal life in the Scriptures with*out Christ,* that is, *by doing them themselves.* But *"this is the record,* that God hath given to us eternal life, and this life *is in His Son,"*—*as we find Him in the Scriptures,* and not in the words of the Scriptures without Him. For they are they that testify of Him. This is their object. Therefore, "he that hath the Son hath life, and he that hath not the Son of God hath not life." 1 John 5:11,12.

"True godliness elevates the thoughts and actions; then the external forms of religion accord with the Christian's internal purity; then those ceremonies required in the service of God are not meaningless rites, like those of the hypocritical Pharisees."—Spirit of Prophecy, vol. ii., p, 219.

MINISTERS OF GOD

A. T. JONES—RH Sept. 29, 1896

FROM the list that the Lord has drawn, in 2 Cor. 6:1–10, it is plain that there is nothing that can ever come into the life of the believer in Christ, but that the grace of God will take it and turn it to the good of the believer, and make it serve only to his advancement toward perfection in Christ Jesus. This the grace of God will do always, and nothing but this, if only the believer will allow the Lord to have his own way in his life; if only he will allow grace to reign. Thus it is that "all things are for your sakes;" and this is how "all things work together for good to them that love God." This is grand. It is indeed glorious. It is salvation itself. This is how the believer is enabled "always" to "triumph in Christ."

This, however, is but half the story. The Lord proposes not only to save him who now believes, but he will use him in ministering to all others the knowledge of God, that they also may believe. We are not to think that the Lord's grace and gifts to us are only for us. They are for us first, that is true. But they are for us first, in order that not only we ourselves shall be saved, but that we may be enabled to benefit all others in communicating to them the knowledge of God. We Ourselves must be partakers of salvation before we can lead others to it, Therefore it is written: "As every man hath received the gift, even so minister the same one to another, as good stewards of the manifold grace of God." And, "all things are of God, who hath reconciled us to himself by Jesus Christ, and hath given to us the ministry of reconciliation."

Thus every man who receives the grace of God, at the same time receives with it the ministry of that grace to all others. Every one who finds himself reconciled to God, receives with that reconciliation the ministry of reconciliation to all others. Here also the exhortation applies, "We…beseech you also that ye receive not the grace of God in vain." Are you a partaker of grace? Then "minister the same" to others; do not receive it in vain. Are you reconciled to God? Then know that he has given to you also the ministry of reconciliation. Have you received this ministry in vain?

If we do not receive the grace of God in vain, if only we will allow grace to reign, the Lord will cause it to be that "in all things" we shall approve "ourselves as the ministers of God." This is the truth. The Lord says it, and it is so. "In *all things* approving ourselves as the ministers of God." That is, in all things we shall be conveying to others the knowledge of God. And thus the Lord proposes not only to cause us always "to triumph in Christ," on our own part, but also to make "manifest the savor of his knowledge by us *in every place.*" That is, he proposes to make known to others *by us,* and in *every place,* the knowledge of himself.

We cannot do this of ourselves. He is to do it by us. We are to co-operate with him. We are to be workers together with him. And when we do thus co-operate with him, then as certainly as we do so, so certainly will he cause us always to triumph in Christ, and will also make manifest the knowledge of himself by us in every place. He can do it, thank the Lord. Do not say, do not even *think,* that he cannot do this by you. He *can* do it by you. He will, too, if only you will not receive his grace in vain; if you will only let grace reign; if you will be a worker together with him.

It is true that there is a mystery about how this can be. It *is* a mystery how God can make manifest the knowledge of himself by such persons as you and I are, in *any* place, much less in *every* place. Yet mystery though it be, it is the very truth. But do we not believe the mystery of God?—Assuredly we do believe it. Then never forget that the mystery of God is God manifest in the flesh. And you and I are flesh. Then the mystery of God is God manifest in you and me, who believe. Believe it.

Do not forget, either, that the mystery of God is *not* God manifest in sinless flesh, but God manifest in sinful flesh. There could never be any mystery about God's manifesting himself in sinless flesh—in one who had no connection whatever with sin. That would be plain enough. But that he can manifest himself in flesh laden with sin and with all the tendencies to sin, such as ours is—that *is* a mystery. Yea, it is the mystery of God. And it is a glorious fact, thank the Lord! Believe it. And before all the world, and for the joy of every person in the world, in Jesus Christ he has demonstrated that this great mystery is indeed a fact in human experience. For "as the children are partakers of flesh and blood, he also himself likewise took part of the same." "*In all things* it behooved him to be made like unto his brethren." And therefore God "made him to be sin for us." "He hath laid on him the iniquity of us all." Thus, in our flesh, having our nature, laden with iniquity, and himself made to be sin, Christ Jesus lived in this world, tempted in all points like as we are; and yet God always caused him to triumph in him, and made manifest the savor of his knowledge by him in every place. Thus God was manifest in the flesh,—in our flesh, in human flesh laden with sin,—and made to be sin in itself, weak and tempted as ours is. And thus the mystery of God was made known to all nations for the obedience of the faith. O, believe it!

And this is the mystery of God to-day and forever—God manifest in the flesh, in human flesh, in flesh, laden with sin, tempted and tried. In this flesh, God will make manifest the knowledge of himself in every place where the believer is found. Believe it, and praise his holy name!

This is the mystery which to-day, in the third angel's message, is again to be made known to all nations for the obedience of the faith. This is the mystery of God, which in this time is to be "finished,"—not only finished in the sense of being ended to the world, but finished in the sense of being brought to completion in its grand work *in the believer.* This is the time when the mystery of God is to be finished in the sense that God is to be manifest in the flesh in every true believer, in every place where that believer shall be found. This is, in deed and in truth, the keeping of the commandments of God and the faith of Jesus.

"Be of good cheer; I have overcome the world,"—I have revealed God in the flesh. Our faith is the victory that has overcome the world. Therefore, and now, "Thanks be unto God, which always causeth us to triumph in Christ, and maketh manifest the savor of his knowledge by us in every place."

KEPT BY THE WORD

A. T. JONES—RH Oct. 13, 1896

In the Christian life everything depends upon the word of God. It is true that God is able, and desires, to keep us from sinning; but this must be done through his word. So it is written, "By the word of thy lips I have kept me from the paths of the destroyer." "Thy word have I hid in my heart, that I might not sin against thee." This is the way that God has appointed, and there is no other way to have this thing accomplished.

Nor is this way appointed merely because he arbitrarily chose that this *should* be the way, and then laid it upon men that this *must* be the way that they should go. His word is the way of salvation and the way of sanctification (Christian living), because this is the way that the Lord does things; because this is the way that he manifests himself. It was by his word that he created all things in the beginning; it is by his word that he creates men anew; and it will be by his word that he will re-create this world and all things pertaining to it. "By the word of the Lord were the heavens made; and all the host of them by the breath of his mouth…For he spake, and it was done; he commanded, and it stood fast." "Being born again,…by the word of God." "And he that sat upon the throne said, Behold, I make all things new…And he said unto me, It is done."

It is not only that the worlds were created by the word of God; but they are also sustained by the same word. "By the word of God the heavens were of old, and the earth standing out of the water and in the water: whereby [by the word of God] the world that then was, being overflowed with water, perished. But the heavens and the earth, which are now, *by the same word* are kept in store." So also it is not only that the Christian is created by the word of God, but by that same word he is sustained, nourished, and caused to grow. God holds up "all things" by his powerful word. And the Christian is among this "all things" no less than any or all the worlds.

There can be no question whatever that all the worlds are held up, and held in their places, by the Lord. But it is not only all the worlds, it is *"all things"* that are held up and held in place by the Lord. And it is as true of the Christian as it is of any star in the firmament or any world on high. Nor can there be any question that the stars and the worlds are held up and held in their courses by the word of the Lord. And no less than this can there be any question that the Christian is held up and held in his right course by the word of the Lord.

This is to be believed and depended upon by every one who professes the name of Christ. You and I can no more hold ourselves up and in the right way than can the sun or the earth. And as certainly as the worlds are dependent upon his word, so certainly is the Christian to depend upon his word. And when this is so, the Christian is kept in the way of the Lord as certainly and as easily as is any planet in the universe. It is written that he "is able to keep you from falling." And he says, "I will uphold thee with the right hand of my righteousness." "Yea, he *shall be* holden up: for God is able to make him stand."

O struggling, failing Christian, is not that word which holds up great worlds able also to hold up you? Trust that word. Depend implicitly upon it. Rest wholly *upon* it; and then you will find rest in it. Trust the Lord to hold you up, just as you trust him to hold up the sun. His word holds up the sun, and his word is over and over to you, "Fear thou not; for I am with thee." "I will uphold thee." I will keep thee, thou art mine. "I will never leave thee, nor forsake thee." I will never leave thee till I have done that thing which I have spoken to thee of.

"The word of God is quick ['living,' R.V.] and powerful." "Powerful" means "full of power." The word of God is living and full of power, to do for you, with you, and in you, all that that word says. Believe that word, trust it; for it is the word of the living God. It is the word of the pitying Saviour. "Receive with meekness the engrafted word, which is able to save your souls." "I commend you to God, and to *the word* of his grace, which is able to build you up." "Let the word of Christ dwell in you richly." You "are kept by the power of God through faith." The power of God is manifested through his word, and therefore it is his powerful word. Faith comes by hearing the word of God; therefore it is the *faithful* word, the word full of faith. Therefore when he says, you "are kept by the power of God through faith," it is only saying in another way, You are kept by the word of God, "unto salvation ready to be revealed in the last time." Believe that word, trust it, and find its keeping power.

THE POWER OF THE WORD–I

A. T. JONES—RH Oct. 20, 1896

"As the rain cometh down, and the snow from heaven, and returneth not thither, but watereth the earth, and maketh it bring forth and bud, that it may give seed to the sower, and bread to the eater: so shall my word be that goeth forth out of my mouth: it shall not return unto me void, but it shall accomplish that which I please, and it shall prosper in the thing whereto I sent it."

The earth can bring forth vegetation only because of the moisture that comes upon it by the rain or the snow from heaven. Without this, everything would fade and perish. So also is it with the life of man and the word of God. Without the word of God the life of man is as barren of power and of good as is the earth without rain. But only let the word of God fall upon the heart as the showers upon the earth; then the life will be fresh and beautiful in the joy and peace of the Lord, and fruitful with the fruits of righteousness which are by Jesus Christ.

Notice, too, it is not *you* who are to do that which he pleases; but, "It shall accomplish that which *I* please." *You* are not to read or hear the word of God, and say, *I* must do that, *I* will do that. You are to open the heart to that word, that *it* may accomplish the will of God in you. It is not *you* who are to do it, but *it*. "It," the word of God itself, is to do it, and you are to *let* it. "*Let* the word of Christ dwell in you."

This is stated in another place thus: "When ye receive the word of God which ye heard of us, ye received it not as the word of men, but as it is in truth, the word of God, *which effectually, worketh* also in you that believe." Thus it is the word of God that must work in you. You are not to work to do the word of God: the word of God is to work in you to cause you to do. "Whereunto I also labor, striving according *to his working,* which worketh in me *mightily*."

The word of God being living and full of power, when it is allowed to work in the life, there will be powerful work wrought in that individual. As this word is the word of God, the power, of which it is full, is only the power of God; and when that word is allowed to work in the life, there will be the work of God manifested in the life—it is his power working mightily. And thus it is *God that worketh* in you, both to will and to do of his good pleasure. "*It* shall accomplish that which I please." Let it.

From these scriptures it is plain that we are expected to look upon the word of God only as *self-fulfilling.* The word of God is self-fulfilling. This is the great truth presented everywhere in the Bible. This is the difference between the word of God and the word of men. And this is just the difference emphasized in the passage that says, "When ye received the word of God,...ye received it *not as the word of men,* but as it is in truth, the word of God, which effectually worketh also in you that believe."

There is no power in the word of a man to do what it says. Whatever may be the man's ability to accomplish what he says, there is no power in the man's word itself to accomplish what he says. A man's word may express the easiest possible thing for him to accomplish, and you may thoroughly believe it, yet it is altogether dependent upon the man himself to accomplish it *apart from his word*. It is not his word that does it. It is he himself that must do it; and this just as really as though he had spoken no word at all. Such is the word of men.

It is not so with the word of God. When the word is spoken by the Lord, there is at that moment *in that word* the living power to accomplish what the word expresses. It is not needed that the Lord employ any shadow of any other means than that word itself to accomplish what the word says. The Bible is full of illustrations of this, and they are written to teach us this very thing,—that we shall look upon the word as the word of God, and not as the word of men; and that we may receive it thus as it is in truth, the word of God, that *it* may work effectually in us the will and good pleasure of God.

"By the word of the Lord were the heavens made; and all the host of them by the breath of his mouth.... For he spake, and it was." "Through faith we understand that the worlds were framed by the word of God, so that things which are seen were not made of things which do appear." At first there were no worlds at all. More than this, there was none of the materials of which the worlds are made. There was nothing. Then God spoke, and all the worlds were in their places. From whence came the worlds, then? Before he spoke, there were none; after he spoke, there they were. Whence, then, did they come? What produced them? What produced the material of which they are composed? What caused them to exist? It was *the word* which was spoken that did it all. And this word did it all, because it was the word of God. There was in that word the divinity of life and spirit, the creative power, to do all that the word expressed. Such is the word of God.

"And this is the word which by the gospel is preached unto you." The word of God in the Bible is the same,—the same in life, in spirit, in creative power,—precisely the same, as that word that made the heavens and all the host of them. It was Jesus Christ who spoke the word at creation; it is he who speaks the word in the Bible. At creation the word which he spoke made the worlds; in the Bible the word which he speaks saves and sanctifies the soul. In the beginning the word which he spoke created the heavens and the earth; in the Bible the word which he speaks creates in Christ Jesus the man who receives that word. In both places, and everywhere in the work of God, *it is the word* that does it.

Let the word of Christ dwell in you richly. Receive it, not as the word of men, but as it is in truth, the word of God, which effectually worketh also in you. Then, "as the rain cometh down, and the snow from heaven, and returneth not thither, but watereth the earth, and maketh it bring forth and bud, that it may give seed to the sower, and bread to the eater: so *shall my word be* that goeth forth out of my mouth: it shall not return unto me void, but it shall accomplish that which I please, and it shall prosper in the thing *whereto I sent it*," "To you is the word of this salvation sent." "And now, brethren, I commend you to God and to *the word* of his grace, which is able [literally, 'full of power'] to build you up, and to give you an inheritance among all them which are sanctified."

THE POWER OF THE WORD–II

A. T. JONES—RH Oct. 27, 1896

We have seen that the power abiding in the word of God is sufficient, only upon the speaking of that word, to create worlds. It is likewise sufficient, now that it is spoken to men, to create anew, in Christ Jesus, every one who receives it.

In the eighth chapter of Matthew it is related that a centurion came to Jesus, "beseeching him, and saying, Lord, my servant lieth at home sick of the palsy, grievously tormented, And Jesus saith unto him, I will come and heal him. The centurion answered and said, Lord, I am not worthy that thou shouldest come under my roof: but *speak the word only,* and my servant shall be healed…. And Jesus said unto the centurion, Go thy way; and as thou hast believed, so be it done unto thee. And his servant was healed in the selfsame hour."

Now what was it that the centurion expected would heal his servant? It was "the word only," which Jesus would speak. And after the word was spoken, what did the centurion depend upon, to what did he look, for the healing power?—It was "the word only." He did not look for the Lord to do it in some ways apart from the word. No. He heard the word, "So be it done unto thee." He accepted that word as it is in truth the word of God, and expected *it*, depended upon *it,* to accomplish that which it said. And it was so. And that word is the word of God to-day as certainly as in the day that it was originally spoken. It has lost none of its power, for that word "liveth and abideth forever."

Again, in John 4:46–52 it is related how a certain nobleman, whose son was sick at Capernaum, came to Jesus at Cana of Galilee, and "besought him that he would come down, and heal his son; for he was at the point of death. Then said Jesus unto him, Except ye see signs and wonders, ye will not believe. The nobleman saith unto him, Sir, come down ere my child die. Jesus saith unto him, Go thy way; thy son liveth. And the man believed the word that Jesus had spoken unto him, and he went his way. And as he was now going down, his servants met him, and told him, saying, Thy son liveth. Then inquired he of them the hour when he began to amend. And they said unto him, Yesterday at the seventh hour the fever left him. So the father knew that it was at the same hour in the which Jesus said unto him, Thy son liveth."

This is the power of the word of God to the man who receives it as it is in truth the word of God. This is the power that "effectually worketh also in you that believe." This is the way that the word of God accomplishes that which he pleases, in those who will receive it, and let it dwell in them. Notice that in both instances the thing was accomplished at the very time when the word was spoken. Notice also that the sick ones were not in the immediate presence of Jesus, but some distance away—the latter was at least a day's journey away from where Jesus was spoken to by the nobleman. Yet he was healed at once, when the word was spoken. And that word is living and full of power to-day, as certainly as it was that day, to every one who receives it as was done that day. It is faith to accept that word as the word of God, and to depend. upon *it* to accomplish the thing that it says. For of the centurion when he said, "Speak the word only, and my servant shall be healed," Jesus said to them that stood around, "I have not found so *great faith,* no, not in Israel." Let him find it now everywhere in Israel.

Jesus says to every one of us, "Now ye are clean through the word which I have spoken unto you." It is *through the* word that this cleansing is wrought. The Lord does not propose to cleanse you in any way apart from his word, but through the word which he has spoken. There, and there alone, are you to look for the cleansing power, receiving it as it is in truth the word of God which effectually worketh in you, and accomplishes that which he pleases. He does not propose to make you pure except by the power and indwelling of his pure words.

A leper said to Jesus, "Lord, if thou wilt, thou canst make me clean." And Jesus answered him, "I will; be thou clean. And immediately his leprosy was cleansed." Are you mourning under the leprosy of sin? Have you said, or will you now say, "Lord, if thou wilt, thou canst make me clean?" The answer is now to you, "I will; be thou clean." And "immediately" *you are cleansed* as certainly as was that other leper. Believe the word, and praise the Lord for its cleansing power. Do not believe for that leper away back there; believe it for yourself here, now, immediately. For the word is to you now, "Be thou clean." Accept it as did those of old, and immediately it worketh effectually in you the good pleasure of the Father.

Let all who have named the name of Christ receive his word to-day as it is in truth the word of God, depending upon that word to do what the word says. Then as Christ loved the church, and gave himself for it, "that he might sanctify and cleanse it with the washing of water by the word, that he might present it to himself a glorious church, not having spot, or wrinkle, or any such thing; but that it should be holy and without blemish," even so it will be now to the glory of God.

LIVING BY THE WORD

A. T. JONES—RH Nov. 10, 1896

"Now the righteousness of God without the law is manifested, being witnessed by the law and the prophets; even the righteousness of God which is by faith of Jesus Christ unto all and upon all them that believe: for there is no difference: for all have sinned, and come short of the glory of God."

The righteousness of God is that which every man is to seek first of all. "Seek ye first the kingdom of God, and his righteousness." And in the way of righteousness there is life. It is impossible to separate the life of God from the righteousness of God. As certainly as you have the righteousness of God, so certainly you have the life of God.

And "*now* the righteousness of God is made known." Now *is at this time,* at this very moment, even while you read. At this very moment, then, the righteousness of God is manifested "unto all, and upon all them that believe." Do you believe in Jesus Christ *now*, at this moment? Do you? If you say, Yes, then "now," at this very moment, the righteousness of God is made known to you and upon you. Do you believe it? The word of God says that it is; do *you* say that it is? And if you do not say that it is, then do you believe the word? When the Lord says plainly to you that his righteousness is "now" manifested unto you and upon you, and you do not say that it is *now* manifested unto you and upon you, then do you really believe the Lord? When he plainly says a thing to you, and you will not say that that thing is true to you, then do you really believe him?

The Lord wants you to say that what he says is so; that it is so "now," at this moment; and that it is so to you and in you. "A new commandment I write unto you, which thing is true in him and in you." When the Lord says a thing, it is true, even though nobody in the world ever believes it. It would be true in him, but not in them. But he wants it to be true in you as well as in himself. And when you acknowledge that what he says is true to you "now," at this moment, then that thing is true in him *and in you.* This is believing God. It is believing his word. This is having his word abiding in you. And, "If ye abide in me, and my words abide in you, ye shall ask what ye will, and it shall be done unto you."

Many people are ready to admit, in a general way, that what the Lord says is so; they will admit that it may be so to other people; but that it is so to themselves, just now, they will not say. Such people do not really know that the word of God is true. "Hast thou faith? have it to thyself before God." If you do not have faith for yourself, faith of your own, you do not have faith at all. If you do not believe the word of the Lord as being true to you personally and *now*, you do not believe it at all; for as you are not living yesterday nor to-morrow, but just now, while it is *now*, so if you do not believe *now*, you do not believe at all. Therefore the word of God is that *now* is the accepted time; *now* is the day of salvation; and, "*Now* the righteousness of God…is manifested, being witnessed by the law and the prophets; even the righteousness of God which is by faith of Jesus Christ unto all and upon all them that believe."

Do you believe in Jesus Christ as your personal Saviour now? You can answer that in one moment; you know that you do. Then this moment thank the Lord that his righteousness is manifested unto you and upon you. He not only says it, but he gives you witnesses to the fact,—it is witnessed by the law and the prophets. That law which you have transgressed, that law that has shown you guilty before God, that very law *"now,"* in view of the manifestation of the righteousness of God, witnesses that you have a just claim to this righteousness, and that you are thereby justified through the faith of Jesus Christ. The prophets likewise witness to this blessed fact. "The moment the sinner believes in Christ, he stands in the sight of God uncondemned; for the righteousness of Christ is his; Christ's perfect obedience is imputed to him." Is not this, then, sufficient to cause you to say *now*, at this moment, if never before, that "*now* the righteousness of God is manifested" unto you and upon you who *now* do believe in Jesus?

"Being justified freely by his grace through the redemption that is in Christ Jesus: whom God hath set forth to be a propitiation through faith in his blood, to declare his righteousness for the remission of sins that are past, through the forbearance of God." Would you rather have the righteousness of God *now* than to have your sins? You say, Yes. Very good. God has "now" set forth Christ Jesus "to declare" to you "his righteousness for the remission of sins that are past." Will you let the sins go *now*, this moment; and take the righteousness which he is set forth purposely to give, and which he *now*, this moment, freely gives? "Being justified freely." "Being" is present tense. "Was" is past; "shall be" is future; but "being" is present. Therefore the Lord says to you and of you who believe in Jesus, "Being [*now*, at this moment] justified freely by his grace through the redemption that is in Christ Jesus…through the forbearance of God."

But the Lord does not drop the subject yet. He emphasizes the present power and blessing of this infinite fact. "To declare, I say, *at this time* his righteousness." First he says that it is "now" that the righteousness of God is manifested unto all and upon all them that believe; then he speaks of all such as "*being* justified freely;" and next he emphasizes it all thus: "To declare, I say *at this time* his righteousness." O poor, trembling, doubting soul, is not this assurance enough that now, at this moment, the righteousness of God is yours? that *now* you are being justified freely by his grace? that *now*, "at this time," righteousness is declared to you for the remission of all your sins that are past?

Is not this enough? It is enough to satisfy the Lord; for he says, "To declare, I say, at this time, his righteousness: *that he might be just, and the justifier of him that believeth in Jesus.*" Then as it is all-sufficient to satisfy the Lord, is it not enough to satisfy you? Will you *now* take the fullness of this blessed "gift of righteousness," which is life, so that the Lord, by seeing the fruit of the travail of his soul, shall be satisfied again, and so, by your rejoicing, be doubly satisfied? This is all he asks of you. For "to him that worketh not, but believeth on him that justifieth the ungodly, his faith is counted for righteousness."

Here is the word of God, the word of righteousness, the word of life, to you "*now*," "at this time." Will you be made righteous by it *now*? Will you live by it *now*? This is justification by faith. This is righteousness by faith. It is the simplest thing in the world. It is simply whether the word of God shall be true in you "now" or not. God spoke to Abraham, "Tell the stars, if thou be able to number them:...1-Ellipsis potential problem;them:...So shallSo shall thy seed be." And "Abraham believed God, and it was accounted to him for righteousness." "Now it was not written for his sake alone that it was imputed to him; but for *us also*, to whom *it shall he imputed,* if we believe on him that raised up Our Lord Jesus from the dead; who was delivered for our offenses, and was raised again for our justification. Therefore being justified by faith, we have peace with God through our Lord Jesus Christ."

"Now," "at this time," it is true; it is true in him. Now, at this time, let it be true in you.

STUDIES IN GALATIANS

A. T. JONES—RH Aug. 29, 1899

GALATIANS 1:3–5

"Grace be to you and peace from God the Father, and from our Lord Jesus Christ, who gave himself for our sins, that he might deliver us from this present evil world, according to the will of God and our Father: to whom be glory forever and ever. Amen."

"Grace be to you and peace from God the Father, and from our Lord Jesus Christ." Such is the salutation in every epistle by Paul, except that to the Hebrews; and, slightly varied, in both by Peter.

Yet it is not by any means a mere form. These epistles have come to us as the word of God, which they are in truth. This salutation, then, though often repeated, yea, even *because* often repeated,—comes to us as the word of God in greeting and full assurance of his favor and peace everlastingly held forth to every soul.

Grace is favor. This word of God, then, extends his favor to every soul who ever reads it, or who hears it.

His very name is Gracious—extending grace. His name is only what he *is*. And what he is, he is "the same yesterday, and to-day, and forever." With him is "no variableness, neither shadow of turning." Therefore by him grace, boundless favor, is always extended to every soul. Oh, that all would only believe it!

"And peace." He is the "God of peace." There is no true peace, but that of God. And "there is no peace, saith my God, to the wicked." "The wicked are like the troubled sea, which can not rest."

But all the world lieth in wickedness, yet the God of peace speaks peace to every soul. For Christ, the Prince of peace, "our peace," hath made both God and man one, having abolished in his flesh the enmity, to make in himself of two—God and man—one new man, *so* making peace "making peace through the blood of his cross." Eph. 2:14, 15; Col. 1:20. "And, having *made* peace through the blood of his cross," he "came and *preached* peace to you which were afar off, and to them that were nigh:" peace to you all. Therefore, always and forevermore, his salutation to every soul is, Peace to thee. And all from God the Father, and from our Lord Jesus Christ!

Oh, that every one would believe it; so that the peace of God, which passeth all understanding, could keep his heart and mind through Christ Jesus.

"Let the peace of God rule in your hearts." *Let* it; that is all he asks of you. Don't refuse it, and beat it back; *let it.*

"Who gave himself *for our* SINS." O brother, sister, sinner, whosoever you be, laden with sins though you be, Christ gave himself for your *sins*. Let him have them. He bought *them—your sins—*with the awful price of his crucified self. Let him have them.

He does not ask you to put all your sins away before you can come to him and be wholly his. He asks you to come, *sins and all,* and be wholly his, *sins and all;* and he will take away from you, and put away forever, *all your sins. He* gave himself for you, *sins and all;* he bought you, *sins and all;* let him have what he bought, let him have his own, let him have *you, sins and all.*

He "gave himself for our sins, *that he might deliver us from this present evil world.* " Notice that to deliver us from this present evil world, he gave himself for our *sins.* That shows that all that there is of this present evil world to each one of us, is *in* our *sins.*

And they were "*our* sins." They belonged to *us. We* were responsible for them. And so far as we were concerned, this present evil world lay in our own personal selves, in our sins. But, bless the Lord, he gave himself for us, sins and all; he gave himself for our sins, ourselves and all; and this he did in order that he might deliver us from this present evil world.

Would you like to be delivered from this present evil world?—Let him have yourself, sins and all, which he bought, and which therefore by full right belong to him. Please do not rob him of what is his own, and so still remain in this present evil world, when at the same time you would like to be delivered from this present evil world. Please do not commit the additional sin of keeping what does not belong to you.

As they were *our* sins, and he gave himself for them, it follows plainly enough that he gave himself *to us* for our sins. Then, when he gave himself for *your* sins, your sins became *his*: and when he gave himself *to you* for your sins, *he* became *yours.* Let him have your sins, which are *his,* and take for them *him,* who is *yours.* Blessed exchange; for in him you have, as your very own, *all* the fullness of the Godhead bodily; and all "according to the will of God." Thank the Lord.

Why should there not be to him "glory forever and ever"? And why should not you and all people say, Amen?

GALATIANS 2:20

A. T. JONES—RH Oct. 24, 1899

"I am crucified with Christ: nevertheless I live; yet not 1, but Christ liveth in me: and the life which I now live in the flesh I live by the faith of the Son of God, who loved me, and gave himself for me."

It may not be amiss to emphasize what this scripture *does* say, by noting what it does not say.

It does *not* say, I want to be crucified with Christ. It does *not* say, I wish I were crucified with Christ, that he might live in me. It *does* say, "I *am* crucified with Christ."

Again: it does *not* say, Paul was crucified with Christ; Christ lived in Paul; and the Son of God loved Paul, and gave himself for Paul. All that is true; but that is *not* what the scripture *says,* nor is that what it means; for it means just what it says. And it *does* say, "*I* am crucified with Christ: nevertheless *I* live; yet not I, but Christ liveth in *me*; and the life which I now live in the flesh I live by the faith of the Son of God, who loved *me,* and gave himself for *me.*"

Thus this verse is a beautiful and solid foundation of Christian faith for every soul in the world. Thus it is made possible for every soul to say, in full assurance of Christian faith, "He loved *me*." "He gave himself for *me*." "*I* am crucified with Christ." "Christ liveth *in me.* " Read also 1 John 4:15.

For any soul to say, "I am crucified with Christ," is not speaking at a venture. It is not believing something on a guess. It is not saying a thing of which there is no certainty. Every soul in this world can say, in all truth and all sincerity, "I am crucified with Christ." It is but the acceptance of a fact, the acceptance of a thing that is already done; for this word *is* the statement of a fact.

It is a fact that Jesus Christ was crucified. And when he was crucified, *we* also were crucified; for he was one of *us,* His name is Immanuel, which is "God with us"—not God with *him,* but "God with *us.*" When his name is *not* God with *him,* but "God with us," and when God with *him* was *not* God with him, but God with *us,* then who was he but *"us"*? He had to be *"us"* in order that God with *him* could be not God with him, but "'God with *us.*" And when he was crucified, then who was it but *"us"* that was crucified?

This is the mighty truth announced in this text. Jesus Christ was *"us."* He was of the same flesh and blood with us. He was of our very nature. He was in all points like us. "It behooved him to be made in all points like unto his brethren." He emptied himself, and was made in the likeness of men. He was "the last Adam." And precisely as the first Adam was ourselves, so Christ, the last Adam, was ourselves. When the first Adam died, we, being involved in him, died with him. And when the last Adam was crucified,—*he* being ourselves, and we being involved in him—*we* were crucified *with him.* As the first Adam was in himself the whole human race, so the last Adam was in *himself* the whole human race; and so when the last Adam was crucified, the whole human race the old, sinful, human nature—was crucified with him. And so it is written: "Knowing this, that *our old man IS CRUCIFIED WITH HIM, that the body of sin* might be *destroyed,* that henceforth we should not serve sin."

Thus every soul in this world can truly say, in the perfect triumph of Christian faith, "I am crucified with Christ;" my old sinful human nature is crucified with him, that this body of sin might be destroyed, that henceforth I should not serve sin. Rom. 6:6. Nevertheless I live; yet not I, but Christ liveth in me. Always bearing about in my body the dying of the Lord Jesus,—the crucifixion of the Lord Jesus, for I am crucified with him,—that *the life also of Jesus* might be made manifest in my body. For I who live am always delivered unto death, for Jesus' sake, that the life also of Jesus might be made manifest in my mortal flesh. 2 Cor. 4:10, 11. And therefore the life which I now live in the flesh I live by the faith of the Son of God, who loved *me,* and gave himself for *me.*

In this blessed fact of the crucifixion of the Lord Jesus, which was accomplished for every human soul, there is not only laid the foundation of faith *for* every soul, but in it there is given the *gift of faith* TO every soul. And thus the cross of Christ is not only the wisdom of God displayed from God to us, but it is the *very power of God* manifested to deliver us from all sin, and bring us to God.

O sinner, brother, sister, believe it. Oh, receive it. Surrender to this mighty truth. *Say* it, say it in full assurance of faith, and say it forever. "I am crucified with Christ: nevertheless I live; yet not I, but Christ liveth in me: and the life which I now live in the flesh I live by the faith of the Son of God, who loved me, and gave himself for *me.* " Say it; for it is the truth, the very truth and wisdom and power of God, which saves the soul from all sin.

GALATIANS 3:10-12

A. T. JONES—RH Dec. 19, 1899

"Christ hath redeemed us from the curse of the law, being made a curse for us: for it is written, Cursed is everyone that hangeth on a tree: that the blessing of Abraham might come on the Gentiles through Jesus Christ; that we might receive the promise of the Spirit through faith."

The curse of the law, all the curse that ever was or ever can be, is simply because of sin. This is powerfully illustrated in Zech. 5:1-4. The prophet beheld a "flying roll; the length thereof...twenty cubits, and the breadth thereof ten cubits." Then the Lord said to him: "This is the curse that goeth forth over the face of the whole earth." That is, this roll represents all the curse that is upon the face of the whole earth.

And what is *the cause* of this curse over the face of the whole earth?—Here it is: "For every one that *stealeth* shall be cut off as on this side according to it; and every one that *sweareth* shall be cut off as on that side according to it." That is, this roll is the law of God, and one commandment is cited from each table, showing that both tables of the law are included in the roll. Every one that stealeth—every one that transgresseth the law in the things of the second table—shall be cut off as on this side of the law according to it; and every one that sweareth—every one that transgresseth in the things of the first table of the law—shall be cut off as on that side of the law according to it.

Thus the heavenly recorders do not need to *write out* a statement of each particular sin of every man; but simply to indicate on the roll that pertains to each man, the particular commandment which is violated in each transgression. That such a roll of the law does go with every man wherever he goes, and even abides in his house, is plain from the next words: "I will bring it forth, saith the Lord of hosts, and it shall enter into the house of the thief, and into the house of him that sweareth falsely by my name: and it shall remain in the midst of his house." And unless a remedy shall be found, there that roll of the law will remain until the curse shall consume that man, and his house, "with the timber thereof and the stones thereof;" that is, until the curse shall devour the earth in that great day when the very elements shall melt with fervent heat. For "the strength of sin" and the curse "is the law." 1 Cor. 15:56.

But, thanks be to God, "Christ hath redeemed us from the curse of the law, being made a curse for us." All the weight of the curse came upon him, for "the Lord hath laid on him the iniquity of us all." He was made "to be sin for us, who knew no sin." And whosoever receives him, receives freedom from all sin, and freedom from the curse because free from all sin.

So entirely did Christ bear all the curse, that, whereas, when man sinned, the curse came upon the ground, and brought forth thorns and thistles (Gen. 3:17, 18), the Lord Jesus, in redeeming all things from the curse, wore the *crown of thorns,* and so redeemed both man and the earth from the curse. Bless his name. The work *is done*. "He *hath* redeemed us from the curse." Thank the Lord. He *was made* a curse for us, because he *did hang* upon the tree.

And since this is all *an accomplished thing*, freedom from the curse by the cross of Jesus Christ is *the free gift* of God to every soul on the earth. And when a man receives this free gift of redemption from all the curse, that roll still goes with him; yet, thank the Lord, not carrying a curse any more, but *bearing witness* to "the righteousness of God which is by faith of Jesus Christ unto all and upon all them that believe: for there is no difference." Rom. 3:21, 22. For the very object of his redeeming us from the curse is "that the blessing of Abraham might come on the Gentiles through Jesus Christ." That blessing of Abraham is the righteousness of God, which, as we have already found in these studies, can come only from God as the free gift of God, received by faith.

And "as many as are of *the works of the law* are under the curse;" and as "Christ hath redeemed us from the Curse of the law," then he has also redeemed us from the works of the law, which, being only *our own works,* are only sin; and has, by the grace of God, bestowed upon us *the works of God,* which, being the works of faith, which is the gift of God, is only righteousness, as it is written: "This is the work of God, that ye believe on him whom he hath sent." John 6:29. This is rest indeed—heavenly rest—the rest of God. And "he that is entered into his rest, he also hath ceased from his own works, as God did from his." Heb. 4:10.

Thus, "Christ hath redeemed us from the curse of the law," and from the curse of our own works, that the blessing of Abraham, which is the righteousness and the works of God, "might come on the Gentiles through Jesus Christ." And all this in order "that we might receive the promise of the Spirit through faith." And "there is therefore now no condemnation to them which are in Christ Jesus, who walk not after the flesh, but after the Spirit. For the law of the Spirit of life in Christ Jesus hath made me free from the law of sin and death." And "what the law could not do, in that it was weak through the flesh, God sending his own Son in the likeness of sinful flesh, and for sin, condemned sin in the flesh: that the righteousness of the law might be fulfilled in us, who walk not after the flesh, but after the Spirit." Rom. 8:1–4.

Thanks be unto God for the unspeakable gift of his own righteousness in place of our sins, and of his own works of faith in place of our works of the law, which has been brought to us in the redemption that is in Christ Jesus, who "hath redeemed us from the curse of the law, being made a curse for us."

GALATIANS 5:3

A. T. JONES—RH Aug. 21, 1900

"For I testify again to every man that is circumcised, that he is a debtor to do the whole law."

"Debtor to do the whole law." It is curious that many, in considering this statement, have made it mark a distinction between two laws, and have made it exclude the law of God from the subject under consideration, by allowing to the word "debtor" only the sense of "obligation."

They know, by the scripture, that it is the whole duty of man to fear God and keep his commandments. They know that there can not be any other scripture to contradict that. They know that every man is under obligation to keep the whole law of God, whether he is circumcised or uncircumcised. And, allowing that this term implies only obligation,—that if he is circumcised, he is under obligation to do the whole law,—they conclude that this must exclude the law of God: they conclude that it must be some law that no person is under any obligation to do unless he be circumcised; and that therefore the "whole law" here under consideration must be only the whole ceremonial law of sacrifices and offerings.

On the other hand, there are those who hold themselves under no obligation whatever to keep the law of God, who bring in this text to support them in their disobedience and opposition. They will have it that only those who are circumcised are under any obligation to keep the law of God, and that it is only by being circumcised that the obligation comes; and they know that they are not under any obligation to be circumcised. From this they argue that they are under no obligation to keep the ten commandments.

But both of these are wrong: both of them fail to see the thought that is in this verse. And the cause of this failure is in their allowing to the word "debtor" only the sense of "obligation."

It is true that the word signifies "obligation." But, in this place, and in every other place in its connection with men's moral obligations, the word has a meaning so much broader and deeper than that of mere obligation that the sense of mere obligation becomes really secondary.

The word "debtor" in this verse—Gal. 5:3—signifies not only that a person is in debt, and under obligation to pay; but that, beyond this, he is overwhelmingly in debt, with *nothing at all wherewith* to pay. If a man is debtor, and so under obligation, to pay one thousand dollars, and yet has abundance, or even only the ability to pay the one thousand dollars, that is easy enough. But if a man is debtor, and so under obligation, to pay *fourteen millions* of dollars ($14,000,000), and has not a single cent wherewith to pay, and is in prison besides, and has no ability whatever to make a cent wherewith to pay his debt, to *that* man the word "debtor" signifies a great deal more than mere "obligation to pay."

And that is precisely the case here. That is the thought in this verse. That is the meaning embodied here in the word "debtor." This because the word "debtor," when used in connection with morals, implies, and can imply, only sin: that the man is a sinner.

This word "debtor" in Gal. 5:3 is precisely the word that is used in Luke 13:4,—"Those eighteen, upon whom the tower in Siloam fell, and slew them, think ye that they were *sinners* above all men that dwelt in Jerusalem?"—where the word "sinners" in the text, is "debtors" in the margin.

It is the word used in the Lord's prayer (Matt. 6:12), "Forgive us our *debts,* as we forgive our *debtors;*" and which, in Luke's version of the prayer, plainly expresses the thought of sin, in the words: "Forgive us our *sins;* for we also forgive everyone that is *indebted* to us." Luke 11:4.

It is the same word also that is used by the Saviour in Luke 7:41,42: "There was a certain creditor which had two *debtors:* the one owed five hundred pence, and the other fifty. And when they had *nothing* [with which] *to pay,* he frankly forgave them both."

It is the same word also that is used in the parable in Matt. 18:23–35. Indeed, from the verse, Luke 13:4, where the word "sinners" is used in the text and "debtors" in the margin, the reference is direct to this parable in Matthew 18. That is the parable in which it is said that when a certain king "had begun to reckon" with his servants, "one was brought unto him, which owed him ten thousand talents."—about fourteen million four hundred thousand dollars,—and he *had nothing* with which to pay, Then the Lord "forgave him the *debt.*" But when the servant found one of his fellow servants who owed him about fifteen dollars, he would not forgive him the debt, but cast him into prison until he should pay the fifteen dollars. Then the king called up his debtor, "and delivered him to the tormentors, till he should pay all that was due unto him. So likewise shall my Heavenly Father do also unto you, if ye from your hearts forgive not every one his brother their *trespasses.*" Matt. 18:23–35.

That thought of delivering the debtor to the tormentors until he should pay all that was due to his lord, belongs with the word; for "the use of the word involves the idea that the debtor is one that must expiate his guilt." And "sin is called 'opheilema,' because it involves expiation and the payment of it as a debt, by punishment and satisfaction."

From these scriptures the attentive reader can begin to see that in the words of Gal. 5:3,—"he is debtor to do the whole law,"—there is far more suggested than that he is merely under obligation to accept the claims of the law upon him, and do his best to meet them. All this shows that he is not only under *obligation* to recognize the binding claims of the law of God, but that he is actually *debtor* to render to that law all the claims that it has upon him. And in this it is further shown that, of himself, he must everlastingly be *debtor;* because he has absolutely nothing wherewith to pay, and of himself has no means of acquiring anything with which to pay.

And this indebtedness lies not only in his obligation to do the law from this time forward, it also lies in obligation to make satisfaction for *all that is past,—for* all the accumulations of the past, up to the present time.

Accordingly, of himself, every man is everlastingly a debtor in all that is implied in this thought in Gal. 5:3, and the kindred texts that we have here cited; because "all have sinned, and come short of the glory of God." And whosoever would be circumcised in order to be saved, and thus seek to be saved by works of self-righteousness, thereby takes upon himself the obligation to pay to the law of God his whole debt, from the beginning of his life unto the end of it. And in that, he also takes upon himself the obligation to *expiate all the guilt* attaching to his transgressions, and accumulated thereby.

That is what it is to be "debtor to do the whole law." That is what is stated in the words: "I testify again to every man that is circumcised, that he is a *debtor* to do *the whole law.*" He is not only debtor; but, by that transaction, he himself voluntarily assumes *of himself* to discharge all that is involved in his indebtedness.

Now it is true that every man in the world is, of himself, that kind of a debtor. It is also true that any man to-day who seeks justification by his own works, even in the doing of the ten commandments, or of anything else that the Lord has commanded, does thereby assume, and bind himself to pay, all that is involved in the indebtedness. But he can not pay. There is not with him the first element of any possibility, in himself, to pay any of the debt. He is overwhelmed and lost.

But, thanks be to God, whosoever has the righteousness *of God* which is by *faith of Jesus Christ,* whosoever depends only *on the Lord Jesus* and that which *Jesus has done,* though he be of himself debtor just like any other man, yet, *in Christ,* he has wherewith *abundantly* to pay *all the indebtedness.* Christ has expiated, by punishment and satisfaction, all the guilt of every soul; and by the righteousness of God which he brings, Christ supplies abundance of righteousness to pay all the demands that the law may ever make in the life of him who believes in Jesus.

Thanks be unto God for his unspeakable gift of the unsearchable riches of Christ. Oh, believe it! Oh, receive it! Poor, overwhelmed, lost "debtor," "buy of me gold tried in the fire, that thou mayest be rich; and white raiment, that thou mayest be clothed." "Yea, come, buy…without money and without price."

GALATIANS 5:16–18

A. T. JONES—RH Sept. 18, 1900

"This I say then, Walk in the Spirit, and ye shall not fulfill the lust of the flesh. For the flesh lusteth against the Spirit, and the Spirit against the flesh: and these are contrary the one to the other: so that ye can not do the things that ye would. But if ye be led of the Spirit, ye are not under the law."

"If ye be led of the Spirit, ye are not under the law;" because "as many as are led of the Spirit of God, they are the sons of God." As sons of God, these have the mind of the Spirit, the mind of Christ; and so, with the mind they "serve the law of God." Accordingly, whosoever is led of the Spirit of God, and thus has the mind of Christ, fulfills the law; because, by that Spirit, there is shed abroad in the heart the love of God, which, in itself, is the fulfilling of the law, in whomsoever has it.

On the other hand, whosoever is *led of the flesh,* and so has *the mind of the flesh,* does *the works of the flesh,* and *so serves the law of sin.*

And the two ways, the way of the Spirit and the way of the flesh, are *always open before every man.* As certainly as the flesh is there, it "lusteth against the Spirit;" and as certainly as the Spirit is there, it "lusteth against the flesh." Whosoever is led of the flesh can not do the good that he would; he serves the law of sin, and so is under the law. But whosoever is "led of the Spirit is not under the law."

And every man is always free to choose which shall be his way—the way of the Spirit, or the way of the flesh. "If ye live after the flesh, ye shall die: but if ye through the Spirit do mortify the deeds of the body, ye shall live." Rom. 8:13.

Note that, in the text of Galatians now under consideration, and its kindred texts in Romans and also in Colossians, it is stated in words, and constantly held in view, that the flesh, in its true, fleshly, sinful nature, is still present with him who has the Spirit of God; and that this flesh is warring against the Spirit.

That is, when a man is converted, and is thus brought under the power of the Spirit of God, he is not so delivered from the flesh that he is actually separated from it, with its tendencies and desires, so that, by the flesh, he is no more tempted, and that with it he has no more contest. No; that same degenerate, sinful flesh is there, with its same tendencies and desires. But the individual is *no longer subject to these.* He is delivered from *subjection to the flesh,* with its tendencies and desires, and is now *subject to the Spirit.* He is now subject to *a power* that *conquers,* brings under, crucifies, and keeps under, *the flesh,* sinful as it is, with all its affections and lusts. Therefore, it is written that "ye *through the Spirit* do mortify the deeds of the body." "Mortify therefore *your members which are upon the earth;* fornication, uncleanness, inordinate affection, evil concupiscence, and covetousness, which is idolatry." Col. 3:5. Note that all these things are there *in the* flesh and would live and reign *if the flesh were to rule.* But since *the flesh itself* is brought *into subjection* to the *power of*

God, through the Spirit, all these evil things are killed *at the root,* and thus prevented from appearing in the life.

This contrast between the rule of the flesh and the rule of the Spirit, is clearly shown in Rom. 7:14–24 and in 1 Cor. 9:26, 27. In the seventh of Romans is pictured the man who is under the power of the flesh, "carnal, sold under sin," who longs to do good, and wills to do good, but is subject to a power in the flesh that will not let him do the good that he would. "For the good that I would I do not; but the evil which I would not, that I do." "I find then a law, that, when I would do good, evil is present with me. For I delight in the law of God after the inward man: but I see *another law* IN MY MEMBERS, *warring against the law of my mind,* and bringing *me* into *captivity to the law of sin* which is *in my members.* O wretched man that I am! who shall deliver me from the body of this death?" That describes the man who is subject to the flesh, "to the law of sin" that is in the members. And when he would break away from the power of the flesh, and would do good, that power still brings him into captivity, and holds him under the dominion of the flesh, the law of sin, which is in his members.

But there is *deliverance from that power.* Therefore, when he cries out, "O wretched man that I am! who shall deliver me from the body of this death?" there is given instantly the answer: "I thank God through Jesus Christ our Lord." There is the way of deliverance; for Christ alone is the Deliverer.

And now this man, though he is thus delivered, *is not delivered from* A CONTEST: he is not put into a condition where he has no fighting to do *with the flesh.* There is a fight still to be carried on; and it is not a make-believe fight: it is not the fighting of a phantom. Here is the man of 1 Cor. 9:26, 27: "So fight I, not as one that beateth the air." What *does* he fight? What *does* he beat? Read: "But I keep under *my body,* and *bring it into subjection:* lest that by any means, when I have preached to others, I myself should be a castaway."

Thus, in the battle that the Christian fights, is *his body,* is *the flesh,* with its affections and lusts. The body is to be, by the Christian, kept under, and brought into subjection, by *the new power,* of *the Spirit of God,* to which he is now subject, and to which he became subject when delivered from the power of the flesh and the law of sin.

This is made yet more expressive by the fuller rendering of the Greek word translated "keep under," in 1 Cor. 9:27: "I *keep under* my body." It means, literally, "to strike under the eyes, hit and beat the face black and blue." Accordingly, Conybeare and Howson translate this passage thus: "I fight not as the pugilist who strikes out against the air; but I bruise my body and force it into bondage."

Thus the seventh of Romans shows *the man* subject to the power of *the flesh* and the law of sin that is in the members, but longing for deliverance. The ninth of first Corinthians shows *the flesh* subject to *the man* through the new power of the Spirit of God. In the seventh of Romans, *the flesh is ruling,* and *the man is under.* In the ninth chapter of first Corinthians, *the man is ruling,* and *the flesh is under.*

And this blessed reversal of things is wrought in conversion. By conversion the man is put in possession of the power of God, and under the dominion of the Spirit of God, so that, by that power, he is made ruler over the flesh, with all its affections and lusts; and, through the Spirit, he crucifies the flesh with the affections and lusts, in his fighting "the good fight of faith."

Men are not saved by being delivered utterly from the flesh; but by *receiving power to conquer,* and *rule over* all the evil tendencies and the desires of the flesh. Men do not develop character (in fact, they never could) by being delivered into a realm of no temptation; but, by *receiving power,* in the field of temptation exactly where they are, *to conquer all the temptation.*

If men were to be saved by being delivered utterly from the flesh just as it is, then Jesus need never have come to the world. If men were to be saved by being delivered from all temptation, and set in a realm of no temptation, then Jesus need not have come into the world. But never, by any such deliverance as that, could man have developed character. Therefore, instead of trying to save men by delivering them utterly from the flesh, just where they were, Jesus came to the world, and *put himself* IN THE FLESH, just where men are; and *met that flesh,* JUST AS IT IS, with all its tendencies and desires; and by the divine power which he brought by faith, he "condemned sin *in the flesh,*" and thus brought to all mankind that divine faith which brings the divine power to man to deliver him from the power of the flesh and the law of sin, just where he is, and to give him assured dominion over the flesh, just as it is.

Instead of Jesus' trying to save men in a way in which they would be limp and characterless, by setting them in a realm of no temptation, he came to man, just where man is, *in the midst of all his temptations.* Jesus came in the *very flesh such as man has:* and *in that flesh,* he met all the temptations known to that flesh, and conquered every one of them; and by that conquest brought victory to every soul in the world. Bless his name.

And every soul can have in its fullness that victory, who will receive and keep "the *faith of Jesus.*" For "this is the victory that overcometh *the world,* even our faith."

GALATIANS 5:22-26

A. T. JONES—RH Oct. 2, 1900

"But the fruit of the Spirit is love, joy, peace, long-suffering, gentleness, goodness, faith, meekness, temperance: against such there is no law. And they that are Christ's have crucified the flesh with the passions and lusts. If we live in the Spirit, let us also walk in the Spirit. Let us not be desirous of vainglory, provoking one another, envying one another."

We have seen somewhat of the essential evil and deceitfulness of the works of the flesh. But, thank the Lord, there is a better picture.

The Spirit of God, which, in his fullness, is freely given to every believer, lusteth against the flesh, so that in him who is led by the Spirit of God the flesh can not do the things that it would. In such the Spirit of God rules, and causes to appear in the life "the fruit of the Spirit," instead of "the works of the flesh."

And though it be true "that they which do such things" as are described in the list of the works of the flesh, "shall not inherit the kingdom of God," yet in the gift of the Holy Spirit, through the grace of Christ, God has made full provision by which every soul, in spite of all the passions, lusts, desires, and inclinations of the flesh, can inherit the kingdom of God."

In Christ the battle has been fought, on *every point,* and the victory has been made complete. He was made flesh itself—the *same flesh and blood* as those whom he came to redeem. He was made in all points like these; he was "in all points tempted like as we are." If in any "point" he had not *been* "like as we are," then, on *that* point he could not possibly have been tempted *"like as we are."*

He was *"touched* with the *feeling* of our infirmities," because he "was in *all* points *tempted* like as *we are.* " When he was tempted, he felt the desires and the inclinations of the flesh, precisely as we feel them when we are tempted. For "every man is tempted, when he is drawn away of his own lusts [his own desires and inclinations of the flesh] and enticed." James 1:14. All this Jesus could experience without sin; because to be tempted *is not sin.* It is only "when lust hath conceived," when the desire is cherished, when the inclination is sanctioned,—only then it is that "it bringeth forth sin." And Jesus never even in a thought cherished a desire, or sanctioned an inclination, of the flesh. Thus, in such flesh as ours, he was tempted in all points as we are, and yet without a taint of sin.

And thus, by the divine power that he received through faith in God, he, *in our flesh,* utterly quenched every inclination of that flesh, and effectually killed at its root every desire of the flesh; and so "condemned sin *in the flesh."* And in so doing, he brought *complete victory,* and *divine power to maintain it,* to every soul in the world. All this he did "that the righteousness of the law might be fulfilled in us, who walk not after the flesh, but after the Spirit."

This victory, in its fullness, is free to every soul in Christ Jesus. It is received by faith *in*

Jesus. It is accomplished and maintained by "the faith *of* Jesus," which he has wrought out in perfection, and has given to every believer in him. For "this is the victory which overcometh *the world,* even our faith."

He "abolished *in his flesh* the enmity" that separated mankind from God. Eph. 2:15. In order to do this, he took *the flesh,* and *must take* the flesh, *in which that enmity existed.* And he "abolished in his flesh the enmity" "for to make," in order to make, *"in himself* of twain," God and the estranged man, "one new man, so making peace."

He "abolished in his flesh the enmity," in order "that he might reconcile both" Jew and Gentile—all mankind who are subject to the enmity—"unto God, in one body by the cross, having slain the enmity *in himself"* Eph. 2:16, margin. "The enmity" was "in *himself,"* by being "in *his flesh."* And there *"in his flesh"* he slew it and abolished it. And he could do this only by its being indeed "in his flesh."

Thus Jesus took upon him the curse, in all its fullness, precisely as that curse is upon mankind. This he did by "being made a curse for us." But "the curse causeless shall not come," and never came. The cause of the curse is sin. He was made a curse for us, because of our sins. And to meet the *curse* as it is *upon* us, he must meet *sin* as it is *in* us. Accordingly, God "hath made him to be *sin* for us, who knew no sin." And this "that we might be made *the righteousness of God* IN HIM." 2 Cor. 5:21.

And though he thus placed himself entirely at the same great disadvantage as are all mankind,—made in all points like us and so, "in all points tempted like as we are,"—yet not a single tendency or inclination of the flesh was ever allowed the slightest recognition, even in thought; but every one of them was effectually killed at the root by the power of God, which, through divine faith, he brought to humanity.

And thus, "as the children are partakers of *flesh and blood,* he *also* HIMSELF LIKEWISE took part of THE SAME; that through death he might destroy him that had the power of death, that is, the devil; and *deliver them who* through fear of death were all their lifetime *subject to bondage.* For verily he took not on him the nature of angels; but he took on him the seed of Abraham. Wherefore in *all things* it behooved him to be *made like unto his brethren,* that he might be a merciful and faithful high priest in things pertaining to God, to make reconciliation for the sins of the people. For in that he himself hath suffered *being tempted,* he is able to succor them that are tempted." Heb. 2:14–18.

And this victory which Christ wrought out in human flesh, is brought by the Holy Spirit to the rescue of everyone in human flesh who to-day believes in Jesus. For by the Holy Spirit the very presence of Christ himself comes to the believer; for it is his constant desire to "grant you, according to the riches of his glory, to be strengthened *with might* by *his Spirit* in the inner man; *that Christ may dwell in your hearts by faith,* that ye, being rooted and grounded in love, may be able to comprehend with all saints what is the breadth, and length, and depth, and height; and to know the love of Christ, which passeth knowledge, that ye might be *filled* with *all the fullness of God."* Eph. 3:16–19.

Thus the deliverance from the guilt of sin and from the power of sin, which holds the believer in triumph over all the desires, the tendencies and inclinations, of his sinful flesh, through the power of the Spirit of God, this is wrought to-day by the personal presence of

Christ Jesus IN HUMAN FLESH in the believer, *precisely as it was wrought* by the personal presence of Christ in human flesh eighteen hundred and seventy years ago.

Christ is ever the same—"the same yesterday, and to-day, and forever." The gospel of Christ is ever the same—the same yesterday, and to-day, and forever. The gospel of Christ to-day is the same that it was eighteen hundred and seventy years ago. *Then* it was "God manifest in the flesh;" and *to-day* it is the *same*—"God manifest in the" *same flesh,* the flesh of sinful men, human flesh, just as human nature is.

That gospel is "Christ in you, the hope of glory,"—Christ in you *just as you are,* sins, sinfulness, and all; for he gave himself for our sins, and for our sinfulness. And you, *just as you are,* Christ has bought, and God "hath made accepted" in him. He *has received you* just as *you are:* and the gospel, "Christ in you, the hope of glory," brings you under the reign of the grace of God, and, through the Spirit of God, makes you so subject to the power of Christ and of God that "the fruit of the Spirit" appears in you, instead of "the works of the flesh."

And the fruit of the Spirit is—

LOVE—the love of God which is shed abroad in the heart by the Spirit of God. And instead of hatred or any of its kin ever being allowed, even in thought, no man can possibly do anything to you that can cause you to do anything but love him. For this love, being the love of God, is "the same yesterday, and to-day, and forever;" and loves not for reward, but for the mere sake of loving: it loves simply because it is love, and *being* only that, it can not *do* anything else.

JOY—is "ardent happiness arising from present or expected good." But in this case, the alternative "or" is excluded; for this joy is ardent happiness arising from present AND expected good; for the cause of it is eternal. Accordingly, it is everlastingly present, and is everlastingly to be expected. And, therefore, it is "exultant satisfaction."

PEACE—perfect peace that rules in the heart—"the peace of God which passeth all understanding," and which *"keeps the heart and mind"* of him who has it.

LONG-SUFFERING, GENTLENESS, GOODNESS, FAITH.—This faith—*pistis,* Greek—is "firm persuasion; the conviction which is based upon *trust,* NOT upon *knowledge* [the faith of "the *heart,*" not of the *head;* the faith of *Christ,* not of the creed]; a firmly relying confidence cherished by conviction, and bidding defiance to opposing contradictions."

MEEKNESS, TEMPERANCE.—Temperance is self-control. Thus, the Spirit of God delivers the man from subjection to his passions, lusts, and habits, and makes him a free man, master of himself.

"Against such there is no law." The law of God is against nothing but sin. In human lives the law of God is against everything that is not the fruit of the Spirit of God. Therefore it is certain that everything in human life that is not the fruit of the Spirit of God is sin. And this is but stating, in another way, the eternal truth that "whatsoever is *not of faith* is sin."

Therefore "if we live in the Spirit, let us also walk in the Spirit." And because we do live in the Spirit and walk in the Spirit, "let us not"—yea, we shall not; yea, we can not—"be desirous of vainglory, provoking one another, envying one another."

CHRISTIAN PERFECTION

A. T. JONES—RH July 18, 25; Aug. 1, 1899

"Be ye therefore perfect." And the song, "Saved to the uttermost," which has just been sung, is sufficient ground for the "therefore," "Be ye therefore perfect." Matt. 5:48. You know that such is the word of God. You know that we are exhorted to "go on unto perfection." Heb. 6:1. You know that the gospel, the very preaching of the gospel which you and I preach, is to "present every man perfect in Christ Jesus." Col. 1:28. Then it is not for us to say that perfection is not expected of us. It *is* expected of us. You must expect it of yourself. I must expect it of myself. And I must not accept anything in myself or of myself that does not meet in perfection the standard of perfection which God has set. What could possibly prevent us from attaining perfection more than to think that it is not expected? I say again, What could possibly prevent you and me from attaining unto perfection more than for us to say that it is not expected that we should be perfect?

Then, as it is settled that the Word says that you and I are to be perfect, the only thing for you and me to consider is *the way*. That is all. Let it be settled by you and by me that perfection, nothing short of perfection as God has set it, is to be expected of you and me; and that you and I will not accept anything in ourselves, in what we have done, nor anything about us, that is a hair's breadth short of perfection as God has set it,—let this be settled by each one, and settled forever,—then inquire only the way, and the thing will be accomplished.

What is the standard, then? What is the standard which God has set?—"Be ye therefore perfect, *even as your Father which is in heaven is perfect.*" The perfection of God is the only standard. And you and I must set ourselves right there, and stand face to face with ourselves, always demanding of ourselves that there shall be perfection such as God's is, in us, and that we will not look with a particle of allowance upon, we will not apologize for, nor excuse, anything in ourselves that is in any conceivable degree short of that perfection.

It is plain enough that we can not be perfect in greatness as God is, nor in omnipotence as he is, nor in omniscience as he is. God is character; and it is perfection of *character* as his is, that he has set for you and me, to which we shall attain, which alone we are to expect, and which alone we are to accept in ourselves. Then when it is God's own perfection which you and I must have, and which alone we will accept of ourselves, and we hold ourselves to that standard always, you can see at once that that will be for you and me only to hold ourselves constantly in the presence of the judgment of God. There is where every one of us expects to stand, whether we are righteous or wicked. Why not stand there, then, and be done with it? It is settled that you and I are to stand at the judgment-seat of Christ, and there every one of us shall be measured by that standard. God "hath appointed a day, in the which he will judge the world in righteousness by that man whom he hath ordained; whereof he hath given assurance unto all men, in that he hath raised him from the dead." Acts 17:31.

The resurrection of Christ is God's pledge to the world that every man shall stand before the judgment-seat of Christ. That is settled. You and I expect it; we preach it; we believe it. Then why not put ourselves there, and stand steadily there? Why wait? Those who wait, and continue to wait, will not be able to stand there. The ungodly can not stand in this judgment; but those who put themselves before the judgment-seat of God, facing the standard of judgment, and hold themselves there constantly in thought, word, and deed, are ready for the judgment any moment. Ready for it?—They have it; they are there; they are passing it; they are inviting the judgment, and all that the judgment brings; they stand there expecting to be passed upon: and only he who does this is safe. The very blessing that comes in that thing is all the reward that any person needs for putting himself *just now* before the judgment-seat. And standing there, what has he to fear?—Nothing. And when all fear is cast out, what is it that does it?—Perfect love. But perfect love can come only by our meeting that perfect standard of the judgment, *in* the judgment, and can be kept only by standing there.

That being settled, let us inquire the way,—the way; that is all. It is settled, then, that *mine* is not the standard. Think of it! "Be ye therefore perfect, *even as your Father* which is *in heaven* is perfect." His perfection is the only standard. Then whose *measurement* of the standard, whose estimate of the standard, is the proper one?—Not mine. I can not measure God's perfection. You remember the verse—perhaps it occurs to you this moment: "I have seen an end of all perfection: but thy commandment is exceeding broad." Ps. 119:96.

No finite mind can measure God's perfection. Then it is settled, so far, that we are to be perfect; our perfection is to be as his perfection is, and according to *his own estimate* of *his own* perfection. Then that takes entirely away from you and me the whole plan, and everything about it as to the doing of it. For when I can not measure the standard, how should I attain to it, even if it were given me to do? Then let it be settled also that as to the *doing* of it, it is put utterly beyond you.

This also was said long, long ago: "I know it is so of a truth: but how should man be just with God? If he will contend with him, he can not answer him one of a thousand.... If I speak of strength, lo, he is strong: and if of judgment, who shall set me a time to plead?"

And when I should come to plead, what then?—"If I justify myself, mine own mouth shall condemn me." If I can measure up myself to the satisfaction of myself, and pronounce the balance settled; when it is set alongside of *his* estimate, my own estimate is so far short that it condemns me utterly. There is in it no basis of justification. "If I say, I am perfect, it [my own mouth] shall also prove me perverse."

"Though I were perfect, yet would I not know my soul: I would despise my life." My own standard of perfection, when set in the presence of *his,* and seen in the light of his, would be so far short that I myself would despise it. "If I wash myself with snow-water, and make my hands never so clean; yet shalt thou plunge me in the ditch, and mine own clothes shall abhor me." Job 9:1, 2, 19–21, 30, 31.

That is as near as we could come to the standard, if it were given to us to do. Then let us forever abandon all idea that perfection is anything that we are to work out. Perfection is that to which we are to attain, nothing but that. God expects it, and he has made provision for it. That is what we were created for. The only object of our existence is to be just that,—perfect with God's perfection. And remember that we are to be perfect with his *character.* His standard of character is to be ours. Yea, his character itself is to be ours. We are not to have one made like it: it itself is to be ours. And that alone is Christian perfection.

Now that we must have that, the whole story is told in three texts. The first one is in the first chapter of Ephesians, beginning with the third verse in order correctly to get the story in the fourth verse:—

"Blessed be the God and Father of our Lord Jesus Christ, who hath blessed us with all spiritual blessings in heavenly places in Christ: according as he hath chosen us in him before the foundation of the world [now notice what he chose us for; this is the object he had before the foundation of the world, in choosing you and me, and bringing us to this hour. Then let us face the issue] , *that we should be holy and without blame before him in love."*

That is his only thought concerning us. That is all that he made us for; that is all we exist for. Then another word right there: When that is so, why shall we not face it? Why shall we not just now meet the object of our existence and be holy and without blame before him in love?

The next text is Col. 1:19-22: "It pleased the Father that in him should all fullness dwell; and, having made peace through the blood of his cross, by him to reconcile all things unto himself; by him, I say, whether they be things in earth, or things in heaven. And you, that were sometime alienated and enemies in your mind by wicked works, yet now hath he reconciled in the body of his flesh through death, TO PRESENT YOU holy, and *unblameable* and *unreprovable in his sight,"*

First: He *made us* for that purpose. By sin we were swung entirely out of that purpose, the whole purpose was frustrated; but he endured the cross: it pleased God thus to do, and it pleased Christ thus to do it, that his original purpose might be fulfilled. The point is, that by his cross he reconciled us, in order that this original purpose might be met in us,—the purpose that he had before the foundation of the world, that we should be holy and without blame before him in love. The blood of Christ, the reconciliation of peace which is brought to the world by Jesus Christ, is in order that HE might *present us holy,—*that HE might do that very thing that he had in mind before the foundation of the world,—that HE MIGHT PRESENT YOU AND ME "holy and unblameable and unreprovable in his sight."

The way to Christian perfection is the way of the cross, and there is no other way. I mean there is no other way for you and me. The way to bring it to us, the only way, was by way of the cross. He came that way, and brought it; and the only way for you and me to get it is by the way of the cross. He has made provision that *he himself* shall do this; we do not come into it at all, for the *doing.*

Now notice (Eph. 4:7-13) what is really done in this, how fully he has supplied the need.

"Unto every one of us is given grace according to the measure of the gift of Christ." Now think. What did the gift of Christ do, so far in our study? It "made peace through the blood of his cross," and reconciled all to God. And it did it to make US what, before the foundation of the world, he designed we should be,—"holy and unblameable and unreprovable in his sight." That is the measure of the gift of Christ in this thing. And it accomplished the purpose for all so far that it opened the way for all. And unto *every one of* US, just now, is given grace according to the same measure. Then what the cross brought TO us, and *put within our reach,* the grace of God GIVES us, and accomplishes in us.

Now let us read right on, and you will see that this is all so, right up to the very word perfection itself: "Unto every one of us is given grace according to the measure of the gift of Christ. Wherefore he saith, When he ascended up on high, he led captivity captive, and GAVE GIFTS unto MEN. And he gave some, apostles; and some, prophets; and some, evangelists; and some, pastors and teachers." *What for?*—"*For* THE PERFECTING of THE SAINTS." Brethren, when those gifts are given for that purpose, what are we doing when we do not face the fact, and long for the gifts, and *pray* for the gifts, and *receive* the gifts, which *accomplish the purpose?* What are we doing otherwise?

"For the perfecting of the saints, for the work of the ministry, TILL"—given for an object; brought to us for a purpose, a defined, distinct, definite purpose; and UNTIL that purpose is accomplished. It is given "for the perfecting of the saints;" and it is given "TILL WE ALL COME in the unity of the faith, and of the knowledge of the Son of God, *unto a* PERFECT MAN, unto the measure of the stature of *the* FULLNESS OF CHRIST."

Thus perfection is the only aim. God's standard is the only one. "Be ye therefore perfect, even as your Father which is in heaven is perfect." We can not measure it; and could not attain to it, if it were given us to do. It is the object of our creation; and when that object was frustrated by sin, he made it possible to all by the blood of his cross, and makes it certain to every believer by the gifts of the Holy Spirit.

Then again I ask, Why should we not constantly face Christian perfection, and accept nothing of ourselves but that?

The 24th of Jude connects directly with what has been read and said: "Now unto him that is able to keep you from falling, and *to present you faultless before the presence of his glory* with exceeding joy, to the only wise God our Saviour, be glory and majesty, dominion and power, both now and ever."

He chose us before the foundation of the world, "that we should be holy and without blame before him in love." By the cross he made it possible to every soul, even when by sin we had lost all chance. And by the cross *he bought the right* "to present you holy and unblameable and unreprovable in his sight." The right to do this belongs only to him. You and I could not do it if it were given to us to do; but the right to do it does not belong to us. When we had lost it, nothing but the cross of Calvary could restore it. And no one *could* pay the price of Calvary but he who did pay it. Then as certainly as only he who paid the price could pay the price that must bring this to us, so certainly the right belongs only to him by right of the cross of Calvary. And no one who has not endured the literal wooden cross of Calvary can ever have any right to take up that task to accomplish it. Only he endured the cross: to him only belongs the task. And there stands the word: He "is able." He "is able…to present you faultless before the presence of his glory." He who is able to endure the cross is able to accomplish all that the cross made possible. So he "is able…to present you faultless before the presence of his glory with exceeding joy"—WHEN? That is the question. When?

[Voices: "Now."]

Precisely; he is the same yesterday, to-day, and forever. He is as able just now as he was then, or as he will ever be.

Yet bear in mind that it is ever true that only *by the way of the cross* does it come to you and to me just now or ever. Let us study the Word that you may see this. Read Rom. 5:21, and then glance through the sixth chapter; for it is occupied with this one story. The last two verses of the fifth chapter of Romans read thus: "Moreover the law entered, that the offense might abound. But where sin abounded, grace did much more abound: that as sin hath reigned unto death, even so might grace reign through righteousness unto eternal life by Jesus Christ our Lord."

Now the comparison, or rather the contrast,—for it is a comparison that amounts to a contrast,—"as" and "even so." "As sin hath reigned." You know how sin reigned. Every one here knows how sin has reigned. Some may know even yet how it reigns. When sin reigned, the reign was absolute, so that it was easier to do wrong than it was to do right. We longed to do right; but "the good that I would I do not: but the evil which I would not, that I do." Rom. 7:19. That is the reign of sin. Then when sin reigned, it was easier to do wrong than it was to do right.

"Even *so* might grace reign through righteousness." When grace reigns, it is easier to do right than it is to do wrong. That is the comparison. Notice: As Sin reigned, *even so* grace reigns. When sin reigned, it reigned against grace, it beat back all the power of grace that God had given; but when the power of sin is broken, and grace reigns, then grace reigns against sin, and beats back all the power of sin. So it is as literally true that under the reign of grace it is easier to do right than to do wrong, as it is true that under the reign of sin it is easier to do wrong than to do right.

So then the way is clear, isn't it? Let us go that way. "That as sin hath reigned unto death, even so might grace reign through righteousness unto eternal life by Jesus Christ our Lord. What shall we say then? Shall we continue in sin, that grace may abound?"

[Voices: "God forbid."]

You say, "God forbid." That is right. Now God has put his forbid, and you endorse it, against sinning that grace may abound. Then has not God put his forbid against *sinning at all*? Do you endorse that? Do you put your endorsement upon God's forbid that you shall sin at all under the reign of grace?

[Voices: "Yes."]

Then doesn't he intend that you and I shall be kept from sinning? And when we know that he *intends* it then we can confidently *expect* it. If we do not expect it, it will never be done.

So then the first verse of the sixth chapter of Romans shows that God intends that we shall be kept from sinning, doesn't it?

What does the second verse say?—"How shall we, that are dead to sin, live any longer therein?" Well, how shall we? Then what does that verse intend?—That we shall not continue at all in sin. Then being dead brings in the burial. Buried with him by baptism into death, and raised to walk in newness of life. *"Knowing this,* that our old man is crucified with him, that the body of sin might be destroyed, that *henceforth we should not serve sin.*" There is the course laid out before us, and it is the way of the cross.

Now notice three things there: Knowing this, that our old man is crucified with him. What for?—"That the body of sin might be destroyed." And what is that for?—"That henceforth we should not serve sin." Unless the body of sin is destroyed, we will serve sin. Unless the old man is crucified, the body of sin is not destroyed. Then the way to be kept from sinning is the way of crucifixion and destruction.

The only question, then, for us each to settle, is, Would I rather be crucified and destroyed than to sin? If with you it is everlastingly settled that you would rather be crucified, and rather meet destruction this moment than to sin, you will never sin. "Crucified with him, that the body of sin might be destroyed, that henceforth we should not serve sin." Then freedom from the service of sin lies only through crucifixion and destruction. Do you choose sin, or do you choose crucifixion and destruction. Will you choose destruction and escape sin? or will you choose sin, and destruction, too? That is the question. It is not an alternative. He who would evade destruction, to escape destruction, meets destruction. He who chooses destruction escapes destruction.

Well, then, the way of destruction by the cross of Christ is the way of salvation. Jesus Christ went to destruction on the cross to bring salvation to you and me. It cost the destruction of the Son of God on the cross, to bring salvation to you and me. Will we give destruction for salvation? Will you? Anybody who fixes it, and holds it in his hand as an everlasting bid, that he gives destruction, every moment of his life, for salvation, will never lack salvation.

But there is where the trouble comes. Destruction is not pleasant; it is not easy—that is, to the old man. To the natural choice, it is not easy to be destroyed; but to him who does it, it is easy. It is easy when it is done, and it is easy to continue it forever when it is done.

When is it that we are to do this? When is it that he presents us faultless before the presence of his glory?— Now: and the only way is the way of destruction. *Now* is the time to choose destruction. Now is the time to deliver up yourself forever to destruction. But if I hold myself back, if I shrink from destruction, then what am I shrinking from? Salvation. For "our old man is crucified with him, that the body of sin might be destroyed, that henceforth we should not serve sin."

Then if I meet some experience that puts me into a pressure that seems like destruction, that is all right; for destruction is what I have chosen, that I may not serve sin. Such a surrender brings Christian pleasantness into the life, for the joy, the lasting peace, and the satisfaction of being kept from sinning, is worth all the destruction that can ever come to you and me. It is worth it. So it is not a hard bargain that is driven; it is the grandest one that ever came to men.

Crucifixion, destruction, and then henceforth not serving sin, there, then, is the way to Christian perfection. Why?—"For he that is dead is freed from sin." Rom. 6:7. Thank the Lord, he that is dead is freed from sin. Then the only question that can ever come in my life or yours is, Am I dead? And if I am not, and something occurs that accomplishes it, freedom from sin is the only consequence; and that is worth all that it costs.

See also the next verse: "Now, if we be dead with Christ, we believe that we shall also live with him." The first verse intends that we shall be free from sin. The second verse intends that we shall be free from sin. The sixth verse says that we are not henceforth to serve sin; the seventh verse says he that is dead is freed from sin; the eighth verse says if we be dead with Christ, we shall also live with him. Where does he live—in righteousness or in sin?

[Voices: "In righteousness."]

Very good. Then it is plain that the first, the second, the sixth, the seventh, and the eighth verses of the sixth chapter of Romans all intend that we shall be kept from sinning.

How about the ninth verse? "Knowing that Christ being raised from the dead dieth no more; death hath no more dominion over him." How was it that death ever had dominion over him at all?—Because of sin—not his own, but ours; for he was made "to be sin for us, who knew no sin." Then death hath no more dominion over him. He has victory over sin and all its consequences forever. Then what does that verse tell you and me? We are risen with him. "For in that he died, he died unto sin once: but in that he liveth, he liveth unto God." Then both the ninth and tenth verses also intend that we shall be kept from sinning.

The eleventh verse: "Likewise reckon ye also yourselves to be dead indeed unto sin, but alive unto God through Jesus Christ our Lord. *Let not sin therefore reign* in your mortal body, that ye should obey it in the lusts thereof." And thus again he intends that we shall not sin.

"Neither yield ye your members as instruments of unrighteousness unto sin: but yield yourselves unto God, as those that are alive from the dead, and your members as instruments of righteousness unto God. For *sin shall not have dominion over you:* for ye are not under the law, but under grace." The reign of grace lifts the soul above sin, holds it there, reigns against the power of sin, and *delivers the soul from sinning.*

"What then? shall we sin, because we are not under the law, but under grace? *God forbid*" Thus from the first verse to the fourteenth of the sixth chapter of Romans, there is preached, over and over, deliverance from sin and from *sinning.* That is great, but there is something still in advance of that. "Let us go on unto *perfection.*"

Listen: "Know ye not, that to whom ye yield yourselves servants to obey, his servants ye are to whom ye obey; whether of sin unto death, or of obedience unto righteousness?" Delivered from the power of sin, to whom did ye yield yourselves?—To God; then you are his servants, set free to the service of righteousness. God does not intend there shall be a blank life in his keeping us from sinning. He intends that there shall be active, intelligent *service;* and that only *righteousness* shall be the result. It is a wonderfully great thing to be made free from sin and to be kept from sinning; it is another wonderfully great thing upon that, to be made the servants of righteousness, so that our service is unto righteousness.

Therefore let every soul echo, "God be thanked, that ye were the servants of sin, but ye have obeyed from the heart that form of doctrine which has delivered you. Being then *made free from sin,* YE BECAME THE SERVANTS OF RIGHTEOUSNESS." Thank the Lord for that! He says you are; and when he says you are, it is so. Thank him for it. Thank him that you are delivered from sin; and thank the Lord that you are the servant of righteousness. He has made you so; for he says so.

But that is not all yet. "I speak after the manner of men because of the infirmity of your flesh: for as ye have yielded your members servants to uncleanness and to iniquity unto iniquity; even so now yield your members servants to righteousness *unto* HOLINESS. For when ye were the servants of sin, ye were free from righteousness." The Lord in this appeals to your experience and mine. "When ye were the servants of sin, ye were free from righteousness." You know that that is so. Take now the complement of it: "What fruit had ye then in those things whereof ye are now ashamed" for the end of those things is death. But now, being made *free from sin*, and *become servants to God*, ye have *your fruit* unto HOLINESS, and the end EVERLASTING LIFE."

We are not the servants of sin, free from righteousness; but we are the servants of righteousness, free from sin. As I have dwelt upon this, and the Lord has fed my soul upon the whole of it, I am reminded every once in a while of an expression of Milton's, where he speaks of the songs of the angels as notes of "measured sweetness long drawn out." This sixth chapter of Romans is one of those notes of measured sweetness long drawn out.

It begins with freedom from sin: that is a great thing. Next upon that, freedom from sinning; and that is a great thing. Next upon that, servants to righteousness; and that is a great thing. Next upon that, unto holiness; and that is a great thing. And upon all, the end, everlasting life; and that is a great thing. Isn't that a note, then of the Lord's, of measured sweetness long drawn out? Oh, receive it, dwell upon it, catch the sweet tones, and let them linger in the soul day and night: it does the soul good.

And there is the way to Christian perfection. It is the way of crucifixion, unto destruction of the body of sin, unto freedom from sinning, unto the service of righteousness, unto holiness, unto perfection in Jesus Christ by the Holy Ghost, unto everlasting life.

Let us look again at the statement that the gifts are for the perfecting of the saints, "till we all come in the unity of the faith, and of the knowledge of the Son of God, unto a perfect man, unto the measure of the stature of the fullness of Christ." There is the pattern. The way that Christ went in this world of sin, and in sinful flesh,—your flesh and mine, burdened with the sins of the world,—the way he went in perfection and to perfection, is the way set before us.

He was born of the Holy Ghost. In other words, Jesus Christ was *born again*. He came from heaven, God's first-born, to the earth, and was *born again*. But all in Christ's work goes by opposites for us; He, the sinless one, was made to be sin, in order that we might be made the righteousness of God in him. He, the living one, the prince and author of life, died that we might live. He whose goings forth have been from the days of eternity, the first-born of God, was *born again*, in order that we might be *born again*.

If Jesus Christ had never been born again, could you and I have ever been born again? No. But he was born again, from the world of righteousness into the world of sin; that we might be born again, from the world of sin into the world of righteousness. He was born again, and was made partaker of the human nature, that we might be born again, and so made partakers of the divine nature. He was born again, unto earth, unto sin, and unto man, that we might be born again unto heaven, unto righteousness, and unto God.

Brother Covert says that makes us as brethren. It does certainly make us as brethren.

And he is not ashamed to call us his brethren, either.

Then he was born again, by the Holy Ghost; for it is written, and was spoken to Mary, "The Holy Ghost shall come upon thee, and the power of the Highest shall overshadow thee: therefore also that holy thing which shall be born of thee shall be called the Son of God."

Jesus, born of the Holy Ghost, born again, grew "in wisdom and stature," unto the fullness of life and character in the world, to where he could say to God, "I have glorified thee on the earth: I have finished the work thou gavest me to do." God's plan and mind in him had attained to perfection.

Jesus, born again, born of the Holy Ghost, born of flesh and blood, as we were, the Captain of our salvation, was *made "perfect* through Sufferings." For "though he were a Son, yet learned he obedience by the things which he Suffered; and *being made perfect*, he became the author of eternal salvation unto all them that obey him." Heb. 2:10; 5:8, 9. Jesus thus went to perfection in human flesh, through suffering; because it is in a world of suffering that we in human flesh must attain perfection.

And while growing all the time, he was perfect all the time. Do you see that? There is where many people misconceive the whole thought of Christian perfection—they think the ultimate is the only measure. It is in God's plan, but the ultimate is not reached *at the beginning*. Look again at the fourth of Ephesians. This is a suggestion, thrown out to you and me, how we may attain to this perfection, "the measure of the stature of the fullness of Christ." I read the thirteenth verse; now couple with that verses 14–16: "Till we all come in the unity of the faith, and of the knowledge of the Son of God, unto a perfect man, unto the measure of the stature of the fullness of Christ: *that we henceforth be no more children*, tossed to and fro, and carried about with every wind of doctrine, by the sleight of men, and cunning craftiness, whereby they lie in wait to deceive; *but* speaking the truth in love, *may grow up into Him in all things*, which is the head, even Christ."

This is to be accomplished in you and me by growth; but there can be no growth where there is no life. This is growth in the knowledge of God, growth in the wisdom of God, growth in the character of God, growth in God, therefore it can be only by the life of God. But that life is planted in the man at the new birth. He is born again, born of the Holy Ghost; and the life of God is planted there, that he may grow up into him" in how much?—"In all things."

You remember that "the kingdom of heaven is likened unto a man which sowed good seed in his field." And "the seed is the word of God." The seed is planted. He realizes that night and day it grows, he knows not how. But that seed is what? It is perfect: for God made it. It sprouts presently. What of the sprout?

[Congregation: "Perfect, too."]

Is it?

[Voices: "Yes."]

But it is not a head of grain; it is not a stalk standing full and strong; it is a mere sprout peeping through the ground. But what of it? Is it not perfect?

[Congregation: "Yes."]

According to the rate of its progress, it is as perfect at that point as it will be when its course is finished, at the point of maturity. Do you not see? Let not that misconception abide any more. Away with it!

When that sprout peeps through the ground, you stoop to look at it. It is a thing to be admired. It is charming, because it is perfect. That is as perfect a blade as ever appeared on earth, but it is a mere spindling thing, barely peeping through the ground. That is all there is of it; but it is perfect. It is perfect, because it is as God made it, God is the only one that had anything to do with it. Do you not see? It is all right. So you and I, born again of that good seed of the word of God,—born by the word of God and the Holy Ghost, born of the perfect seed,—when that seed sprouts and grows, and begins to appear among men, people see the characteristics of Christ. And what is he?—Perfect. Then what is the Christian right there?

[Congregation: "Perfect."]

If we be born again through the power of Jesus Christ, and God himself directs the work, what will that be which appears?—It will be perfect. And that is Christian perfection *at that point*. Jesus Christ presents you holy, unblameable, and unreprovable, before the throne *at that point*.

That sprout grows and stands above the ground; presently another blade shoots off; there are two of them, and each is just as handsome as the other. The third one appears; it is now a stalk, and still grows. It now presents another picture altogether from that which it presented at first. Another picture indeed, but no more perfect than before. It is nearer to ultimate perfection, nearer to God's accomplished purpose; but, though nearer to ultimate perfection, it is no more perfect, as it stands now, than it was the moment that it peeped through the ground.

In time it grows to its full height. The head is full-formed. The bloom appears upon it. It is more beautiful on account of it. And at last appears the full head of grain, perfect; and the grains of wheat, each one perfect. The work, God's work, is finished upon it. It is *perfected*. It has attained unto perfection according to God's mind when he started it.

That is Christian perfection. It comes by growth. But the growth can be only by the life of God. And the life of God being the spring, it can grow only according to God's order. Only he can shape the growth. Only he knows, in perfection, the pattern. Christ is the pattern. God knows perfectly the pattern; and he can cause us to grow in perfection according to that pattern; because the same power, the same life, is in this growth that was in the growth of the original pattern, Jesus Christ.

And as Jesus began, at his birth, as a little child in human flesh, and grew up and finished the work that God had given him to do; so you and I, born again, growing up in him in all things, come presently to the day when we, as did he, shall say, and say in righteousness, "I have glorified thee on the earth: I have finished the work thou gavest me to do." For it is written, "In the days of the voice of the seventh angel, when he shall begin to sound, the mystery of God should be finished." We are in that day, We have that mystery given to us to give to the world. It is to be finished for the world; and it is to be finished in those who have it.

But what is the mystery of God? "Christ in you, the hope of glory." "God…manifest in the flesh." Then *in these days* that mystery is to be finished in one hundred and forty-four thousand people. God's work in human flesh, God being manifested in human flesh, in you and me, is to be finished. His work upon you and me is to be finished. We are to be perfected in Jesus Christ. By the Spirit we are to come unto a *perfect man,* unto the measure of the stature of the fullness of Christ.

Is not that worth having? Is not the Lord's way a good way unto perfection? Oh, then, "leaving the principles of the doctrine of Christ, LET US GO ON UNTO PERFECTION; not laying again the foundation of repentance from dead works, and of faith toward God, of the doctrine of baptisms, and of laying on of hands, and of resurrection of the dead, and of eternal judgment." He has freed us from the unstable foundation that we had when in sin. Let the only foundation be that of the service of righteousness unto holiness, and the end, everlasting life.

And to every soul who will face the Judgment, and hold himself in the presence of the Judgment, surrendering himself to crucifixion and destruction, that thing will be accomplished in God's own way, and in the short time in which he has promised to bring us unto righteousness. Then it is only God, God's estimate, his standard, and Christ the pattern, and his the work, always, in all things, everywhere and forever! Then be of good cheer. Let it be Christ first, last, and all the time.

We invite you to view the complete
selection of titles we publish at:

www.TEACHServices.com

Scan with your mobile
device to go directly
to our website.

Please write or email us your praises, reactions, or
thoughts about this or any other book we publish at:

P.O. Box 954
Ringgold, GA 30736

info@TEACHServices.com

TEACH Services, Inc., titles may be purchased in bulk for
educational, business, fund-raising, or sales promotional use.
For information, please e-mail:

BulkSales@TEACHServices.com

Finally, if you are interested in seeing
your own book in print, please contact us at

publishing@TEACHServices.com

We would be happy to review your manuscript for free.

www.ingramcontent.com/pod-product-compliance
Lightning Source LLC
Chambersburg PA
CBHW080521110426
42742CB00017B/3197